EDITH WHARTON

Women Writers

General Editors: *Eva Figes* and *Adele King*

Published titles:

Collette, Diana Holmes
Emily Dickinson, Joan Kirkby
Edith Wharton, Katherine Joslin

Forthcoming

Jane Austen, Meenakshi Mukherjee
Elizabeth Barrett Browning, Marjorie Stone
Ivy Compton Burnett, Kathy Gentile
George Eliot, Kristin Brady
Mrs Gaskell, Jane Spencer
Katherine Mansfield, Diane DeBell
Christina Rossetti, Linda Marshall
Jean Rhys, Carol Rumens
Stevie Smith, Romana Huk
Muriel Spark, Judith Sproxton
Gertrude Stein, Jane Bowers
Virginia Woolf, Clare Hanson

Further titles are in preparation

Women Writers

EDITH WHARTON

Katherine Joslin

St. Martin's Press   New York

First published in the United States of America in 1991

Printed in Hong Kong

ISBN 0–312–05792–X

Library of Congress Cataloging-in-Publication Data
Joslin-Jeske, Katherine, 1947–
    Edith Wharton / Katherine Joslin
        p.   cm. — (Women writers)
    Includes bibliographical references.
    ISBN 0–312–05792–X
    1. Wharton, Edith, 1862–1937 — Criticism and interpretation.
    2. Women and literature — United States — History — 20th century.
    I. Title   II. Series
    PS3545.H16Z685   1991
    813′.52 — dc20
                                                    90–48427
                                                         CIP

Contents

Editors' Preface   vi

Acknowledgements   vii

1 Edith Wharton's Life   1

2 Edith Wharton's Fiction   28

3 *The House of Mirth* and the Question of Women   49

4 *The Custom of the Country* and the Atlantic's Call   70

5 *The Age of Innocence* and the Bohemian Peril   89

6 *The Mother's Recompense*: Spectral Desire   108

7 Edith Wharton and the Critics   128

Notes   143

Bibliography   151

Index   154

Editors' Preface

The study of women's writing has been long neglected by a male critical establishment both in academic circles and beyond. As a result, many women writers have either been unfairly neglected or have been marginalised in some way, so that their true influence and importance has been ignored. Other women writers have been accepted by male critics and academics, but on terms which seem, to many women readers of this generation, to be false or simplistic. In the past the internal conflicts involved in being a woman in a male-dominated society have been largely ignored by readers of both sexes, and this has affected our reading of women's work. The time has come for a serious reassessment of women's writing in the light of what we understand today.

This series is designed to help in that reassessment.

All the books are written by women because we believe that men's understanding of feminist critique is only, at best, partial. And besides, men have held the floor quite long enough.

EVA FIGES
ADELE KING

Acknowledgements

Many organizations and people have assisted me in my work on Edith Wharton. I am grateful to the Alumnae of Northwestern University for a fellowship that allowed me to travel to the Beinecke Library at Yale University to read Wharton's papers and to the staff at the Beinecke for their assistance in locating material. I am also grateful to Western Michigan University for a Faculty Research Support Grant that gave me time to complete this book. Many members of the Edith Wharton Society have also helped to guide my research and thinking about Wharton; I thank them all.

Individually, I would like to thank Carl Smith, Harriet Gilliam, and especially Harrison Hayford at Northwestern University for their reading of early drafts of my material and Edward Galligan and Clare Goldfarb at Western Michigan University for their advice on sections of my later work. The comments and suggestions of Eva Figes and Adele King have greatly helped me give shape to my argument. I thank them both for their work.

My special thanks go to my husband and colleague Thomas Bailey, whose culinary creations, no less than his literary insights, have sustained my work.

To my daughter Emily

1 Edith Wharton's Life

I had written short stories that were thought worthy of preservation! Was it the same insignificant *I* that I had always known? Any one walking along the streets might go into any bookshop, and say, "Please give me Edith Wharton's book," and the clerk, without bursting into incredulous laughter, would produce it, and be paid for it, and the purchaser would walk home with it and read it, and talk of it, and pass it on to other people.

— Edith Wharton, *A Backward Glance*

Edith Wharton awoke in the morning before her husband and guests. With the morning sun over her shoulder, free from the restricting stays of fashionable female clothing, she sat alone, propped upright in bed, writing page after page in pencil and tossing them to the floor. From as early as six to as late as eleven, each morning, every morning, she wrote novels, novellas, short stories, poetry, travel books, social and aesthetic commentary, autobiography and literary criticism. Her secretary collected the pages, arranged them, sent them to be typed, and returned them the next morning for revision; often Wharton revised five or six times before showing her work to others. During those same morning hours, as her friends marvelled, she ordered meals for the day, accepted phone calls, managed her large household with an eye to every detail. After a full morning of work, she faced the remainder of her day with equal energy. She dressed, wandered through her

1

well-tended grounds, giving orders to her gardeners, later
changed into a fresh dress for lunch with her husband and
friends, then often motored in the afternoon, wrote several
letters, read avidly, and dined in the evening as elegantly
and freely as any other woman of her social class.

She belonged to an aristocratic New York family with
ancestry stretching back nearly three hundred years to
colonial times. The family wealth grew from mercantile
roots, generations of Newbolds and Joneses bent on making money and acquiring property. Although her parents
despised countrymen with aristocratic pretensions, they
clearly belonged to the American élite. Edith Jones was
born into a New York social group, known as "The 400"
that being, according to legend, the number of people who
could fit comfortably into Mrs Astor's ballroom. As a child
of American aristocracy (nearly an oxymoron for the fledgling Eastern moneyed class), she grew up in what she later
called "a kind of hieroglyphic world, where the real thing
was never said or done or even thought" (*AI*, 45).

Her role, as a daughter of the "tribe", was to learn the
intricate pattern of social manners, mores, rituals with a
finely tuned awareness of nuance and subtlety. Taught by
her mother and grandmother to see herself in relation to
her society, Edith learned, as other girls did, that identity
is bound to what she later called "the web of customs,
manners, culture" elaborately spun about the self.
Although she later rebelled against the norms of behavior
for females in American society, she retained the notion
that the essence of the self is inextricably bound to the
world around the individual. Later in the role of realist
writer and novelist of manners Wharton decoded her
society, revealing not only the surface manners, but the
various layers of the unuttered, half uttered, or unutterable
meaning that her society had trained her to conceal. Her
writing, the books themselves, made her, in her own mind,
"worthy of preservation" – a "significant *I*". The "I" of

the writer is also the "eye" of the creative mind; as Percy
Lubbock put it, "the young hawk looked out of her eyes."
Her hawklike intelligence – what Wallace Stevens called
"the evilly compounded, vital I" of the writer – peered
sharply into the culture surrounding it.

Although her world provided a rich backdrop for fiction,
it produced few male or female writers. Indeed, any literary talent drew the ridicule of her clan. "For my parents
and their group, though they held literature in great
esteem, stood in nervous dread of those who produced
it," she claimed in her 1934 autobiography *A Backward
Glance* (68). Exceptions included Washington Irving and
Longfellow, who were gentlemen despite their literary
careers, but Herman Melville, a cousin of the prominent
New York family, was banished along with Edgar Allan
Poe for "deplorable Bohemianism". A novelist threatened
the New York clan because they did not want to be
unmasked, especially by one of their own. In 1929 *The
New Yorker* critic Janet Flanner explained Wharton's literary relationship to her Old New York society:

As a talented pioneer of professionalism among the
domestic women of her class, absolution might have
come with the dignity of her fame, had not Mrs. Wharton
discovered her sinful skill at sketching from life . . . many
of her contemporaries felt they had unconsciously sat
across the space of years for too many of her portraits.[1]

Such skill was indeed "sinful" to a society that prided itself
on maintaining a smooth, unblemished and thoroughly
inaccurate public face. According to Wharton, Old New
York eyed authorship "as something between a black art
and a form of manual labor" (*BG*, 69), both activities
beyond the pale of social respectability. Edith Jones
Wharton, the probing realist and able satirist, practiced

a "black art" as threatening to her clan as that of Melville
or Poe and, in its nearness, perhaps more frightening.

She told and retold her life story in letters, conver-
sations, at times in diaries, over the course of her life;
and, on occasion, she tried public autobiography, a difficult
genre for any woman. In *Women's Autobiography* (1980),
Estelle Jelinek collected essays that search through the
pattern of female as opposed to male narratives and find
that the woman's story seems, in that comparison, atypical.
Male autobiographies often tell the story of autonomous,
heroic selfhood; female ones, by contrast, more often tell
the story of relational, shared selfhood. The male tends
to cast himself as a hero on a quest that leads to success;
he sees himself as a representative of his era, a model
worthy of respect; his story moves in chronological order.
Women, by contrast, have told a very different story, one
that emphasizes the self in relation to others, often detailing the lives of others around them, rather than their own.
The female is more often self-conscious, unsure of herself
as a model, anxious to convince readers of her self-worth.
Jelinek found that the form, as well as the content, differs
drastically from male narratives; the woman's story is not
orderly, chronological, and progressive, but rather irregu-
lar, disconnected and fragmentary.

Edith Wharton's attempts to tell her own story fit the
formula Jelinek describes. She tried first in an essay "Life
and I" (*c.* 1920), a fragment not published until 1990;[2]
later she wrote another autobiographical essay that was
published posthumously as "A Little Girl's New York"
(1938). The longer public version of her autobiography
A Backward Glance, seems an odd book until one sees
it in the light of female narratives. She tells the story of
the relational, not the autonomous self.

Wharton's family story is, as she explains, by necessity
the story of her extraordinarily wealthy patrilineage, made
up of "[t]he Schermerhorns, Joneses, Pendletons, on my

father's side, the Stevenses, Ledyards, Rhinelanders on my mother's, the Gallatins on both" (*BG*, 11). She dwells on her great-grandfather, Major General Ebenezer Stevens, born in 1751 in Boston. Private and public records mark the achievements of his life, a military hero involved in the Revolutionary War, the Boston Tea Party, the War of 1812. His story fits accounts of male lives, mirroring the era, embodying masculine heroism. When she begins to tell the story of the women in her family, however, she has no public or even private record, few personal stories handed down from one generation to another, little to weave into the cloth of history but threads from their portraits, whatever they were able to "tell" from the pose and gesture captured by the artist. Such women, Wharton notes, were " 'a toast' and little else" (*BG*, 15).

A woman's story, the traditional tale, given in fiction and biography and autobiography is shaped, as all stories are, by convention. As Carolyn Heilbrun elegantly argues in *Writing a Woman's Life* (1988):

> What matters is that lives do not serve as models; only stories do that. And it is a hard thing to make up stories to live by. We can only retell and live by the stories we have read or heard. We live our lives through texts. They may be read, or chanted, or experienced electronically, or come to us, like the murmurings of our mothers, telling us what conventions demand. Whatever their form or medium, these stories have formed us all; they are what we must use to make new fictions, new narratives.[3]

According to Heilbrun female biography and autobiography have only begun to come of age since the 1970s. Before that time women eschewed power or control and therefore could not write heroic narratives about their lives.

Typical of the traditional female text, Wharton's own life story does little to establish her as a major American writer or to chronicle her literary successes. Instead she dwells on the influence and accomplishments of others, mainly her male forebears and friends, as though that story of the female attachment to the male is the only one she can tell. *A Backward Glance* begins, not with her birth in 1862, but with the three-year-old version of Edith Jones, taking a walk with her father, from his daughter's point of view a regal figure:

> It was always an event in the little girl's life to take a walk with her father, and more particularly so today, because she had on her new winter bonnet, which was so beautiful (and so becoming) that for the first time she woke to the importance of dress, and of herself as a subject for adornment – so that I may date from that hour the birth of the conscious and feminine *me* in the little girl's vague soul. (*BG*, 2)

The story she begins to tell is one already available to her. She, as adorned female, goes off into the world on the arm of a handsome, able, powerful male, who will serve as her escort and guide. In the conventions of her day, she would be handed by the father to a suitable mate, a husband who would continue to offer her masculine wisdom and security. And that would be, more or less, the end of her story. But Edith Jones Wharton, though she did marry, never did fit the culturally constructed tale of female success and happiness. Her story was quite different.

In her autobiography, Edith Wharton wrote a meandering tale that moves away from her in several directions. In her retelling of the story, her favorite childhood activity was what she called "making up": that is to suggest, she was always a writer. Yet the rest of her tale shows her terrible doubts about her genius and abilities. Very soon, the story leaves Edith Wharton and her career behind, ending curiously with eulogies to Henry James, Howard Sturgis, Geoffrey Scott. The movement away from herself, her talent, her career toward her memories of her friends, mostly men, does what women's narratives usually do: it marginalizes her as a writer. Her story, in fact, ends abruptly somewhere before 1920 (the chronology is fuzzy) although she is still alive and writing the autobiography in the 1930s. What are we to do with the last fifteen years?

If we look again at the story of Edith Jones Wharton, the American patrician who wrote perhaps the most thorough fictive studies of American culture, we see that she was all along a writer, from earliest childhood onward. And if we look at that life in the context of women's history, placing a woman's life at the center rather than at the margin of male culture, then we see her life as typical of the lives of women of her era.

Throughout her childhood, she prepared for her career. Her favorite anecdotes about her childhood placed her in the nursery, pacing back and forth, "making up" stories, pretending to read aloud from the pages of a book she could not read and could hardly lift.

> At any moment the impulse might seize me; and then, if the book was in reach, I had only to walk the floor, turning the pages as I walked, to be swept off full sail on the sea of dreams. The fact that I could not read added to the completeness of the illusion, for from those mysterious blank pages I could evoke whatever my fancy chose. (*BG*, 34)

The third child, born long after her brothers, she spent much of her time alone. As an antidote to her solitude, Edith's parents, eventually alarmed by her imaginative play, "called in the aid of toys & play-mates" to distract her. Her desire, at such times, was to retreat to her mother's bedroom alone and pour out "the accumulated floods of pent-up eloquence." Such moments of escape brought "exquisite relief" from the pressure to be like other children. Her "making up" continued as she grew older and could read and write. Although she claimed her mother refused her paper to write on, she apparently wrote many stories; a few survive.

In 1874 when she was twelve, she began a story with the words, "'Oh, how do you do, Mrs. Brown?' said Mrs. Tompkins. 'If only I had known you were going to call I should have tidied up the drawing room'" (*BG*, 73). The decidedly realistic tone of her fiction drew a sour response from her mother who pointed out to her that drawing rooms are "always tidy". Lucretia's earnestness about social propriety, her insistence on a public façade, her desire to maintain the ritual of unuttered truth, becomes the target of her daughter's often brutal irony. The novels and stories that Edith would later write chronicle such deceptions, marking the distance between what is claimed and what is true. Three years later, she wrote a rather lengthy (about thirty thousand words) novella, entitled *Fast and Loose*, under the pseudonym David Olivieri and playfully wrote critical reviews of the work, calling its author amateurish. It is a novel of manners in the style and tone of much of her later work. The heroine Georgie Rivers, forced to choose between love and money, rejects the former, her fiancé Guy Hastings, in favor of the latter, the wealthy and much older Lord Breton. His death allows her a reunion with Guy, but her subsequent pneumonia causes her own death and thus denies the couple a happy ending.

Such tales of imperfect drawing rooms and thwarted love move in the direction of Wharton's mature fiction. As with her early stories, her later fiction reveals fate to be the intricate working out of personal desire amid social expectation, a painful compromise more often than not. The individual is inextricably caught in what Wharton called "the web of customs, manners, culture" elaborately spun about the social group. Although her protagonists long for autonomous selfhood, for what Lawrence Selden in *The House of Mirth* calls "the republic of the spirit", Wharton depicts them instead in their social relations, rarely able to thrive outside the culture which has produced them. The clash between material goals and higher values sounds throughout her major novels: *The House of Mirth* (1905), *The Fruit of the Tree* (1907), *The Custom of the Country* (1913), *The Age of Innocence* (1920) and in later, lesser known novels, *The Mother's Recompense* (1925), *The Children* (1928). Her reluctance, not to say refusal, to allow a happy ending has become one of the most controversial characteristics of her fiction, haunting as it does the endings of the society novels listed above, as well as her renderings of the lives of the poor *Ethan Frome* (1911), *The Bunner Sisters* (written in 1892, published in 1916) and *Summer* (1917).

She began writing poetry early, although it is fair to say that she was never much of a poet. Her mother actually selected several poems in 1878 and had them privately published in Newport, Rhode Island by C. E. Hammett, Jr. The following year Allen Thorndike Rice wrote to Longfellow about her, including samples of her verse. He noted that the young Edith Jones, at sixteen, belonged to a fashionable social group little inclined to urge her toward poetry and enlisted the poet's aid in giving her the encouragement she would need if she were to pursue art. Longfellow sent the verses to William Dean Howells at the *Atlantic Monthly* where one of them was published. Two others were published the next year in the New York *World*. These were heady accomplishments for a seventeen-year-old girl and did indeed feed her taste for the muses.

While Edith continued to read the volumes in her

father's library and to write poetry and prose of her own, her parents began to worry. They preferred that their daughter follow the conventional female text by marrying, having children, accepting the social responsibilities of women of her class. For that reason, they introduced her to society at seventeen (in much the same way they had provided toys and playmates earlier) to stimulate her social desire and stifle her literary talent. She began with an aborted engagement to Harry Stevens, whose mother disapproved of the match. Then Edith Jones found herself attracted to Walter Berry (a man she would much later, after his death, call the love of her life), although he never proposed. Her father died suddenly when she was nineteen, and her mother continued to urge that she follow society's determined course.

As a wealthy, naïve young woman Edith Jones supposedly needed the power and security of an even wealthier, certainly more worldly man. Theodore "Teddy" Wharton, though to Lucretia's liking, was not Edith's intellectual equal. Thirteen years her senior, from a wealthy Boston family, Teddy seemed to offer Edith the socially sanctioned route to female happiness; they married in 1885. His wealth freeing him from the necessity of finding a vocation, Teddy loved to travel, ride horses and hunt. Early in their marriage they travelled, as R.W.B. Lewis points out in his biography, even beyond their budget, settled in fashionable New York with summers in Newport and accepted their allotted social roles.[4] Many accounts, however, exist of their marital problems. Edith showed early and persistent signs of depression and apathy. Her condition was first associated with asthma, an illness exaggerated, interestingly, by close proximity to Teddy and Newport society. As she later told the story, their marriage was not consummated for weeks; and, apparently, sleeping in the same room with her husband made breathing difficult for her.

The story of Edith Wharton's psychological illness, variously labelled "hysteria" or "neurasthenia", mirrors the disease, even dis-ease, of her era. If we look at women's history, we see her as typical of white, leisure-class, intellectual American women of her day. In 1908 she recalled this period of ill health in a letter to her friend Sara Norton: "for *twelve years* I seldom knew what it was to be, for more than an hour or two of the twenty-four, without an intense feeling of nausea, and such unutterable fatigue that when I got up I was always more tired than when I lay down" (*Letters*, 139–40). By her own account, the illness lasted from the late 1880s until nearly 1900, consumed the best years of her youth, and left an "irreparable shade" on her life.

She was first treated by Dr McClellan, a colleague of S. Weir Mitchell, who treated many prominent American women in the late nineteenth century, among them Jane Addams (whose illness lasted eight years), Charlotte Perkins Gilman (whose short story "The Yellow Wallpaper" illustrates the adverse effects of Mitchell's treatment), Winifred Howells (whose illness proved to be physiological), and Alice James. The strains of modern civilization and education were considered to be particularly acute for the frail female mind and body; the "rest cure", therefore, aimed at calming the mind and fattening the body. The patient was removed from her normal surroundings, placed in bed, massaged in lieu of exercise, given stimulating electric shock treatments, and forced to eat large amounts of food.

The patients were all well-educated women from well-to-do families. Education was a burden for such women, not because they were frail, but because they were expected to remain within the home, playing the part of moral, innocent, nurturing "angels". Many young women constrained there found little use for the knowledge they had acquired in public and private educations. As Jane Addams explained the situation in 1892, "I have seen young girls suffer and grow sensibly lowered in vitality in the first years after they leave school. In our attempt to give a girl pleasure and freedom from care we succeed, for the most part, in making her pitifully miserable."[5] Seclusion and inactivity failed to remedy Jane Addams' malady and, likewise, drove Charlotte Perkins Gilman into greater depression. She returned home from her treatment with the following prescription from Mitchell:

> Live as domestic a life as possible. Have your child with you all the time . . . Lie down an hour after each meal. Have but two hours' intellectual life a day. And never touch pen, brush or pencil as long as you live.[6]

Such a regimen, *always* with her child and *never* with her pen, drove Gilman, a social thinker and writer by inclination and education, into even deeper depression. Gilman described her "cure" in her autobiography *The Living of Charlotte Perkins Gilman* (1935):

> I went home, followed those directions rigidly for months, and came perilously near to losing my mind. The mental agony grew so unbearable that I would sit blankly moving my head from side to side – to get out from under the pain. Not physical pain, not the least 'headache' even, just mental torment, and so heavy in its nightmare gloom that it seemed real enough to dodge.

Mitchell's prescription caused such frustration, especially among intelligent, educated, ambitious women because it forced passivity on them. At the very time that these women sought new occupations, he urged their acceptance of traditionally sanctioned, leisure-class inactivity. Wharton, in her illness very much like her "hysterical" cohorts, needed activity, especially intellectual activity.

Edith Wharton, the adult, craved what Edith Jones, the child, had needed: a place to escape and "make up" stories. In spite of the social imperative to be vocationless, Wharton resumed her story telling (after her early literary successes, in fact, S. Weir Mitchell himself wrote to her, praising her work). The novella *The Bunner Sisters*, her most convincing portrait of poverty, was written in this period, along with several short stories, including "Mrs Manstey's View", her first published story, and her second, "The Fullness of Life". Her first published book came in 1897, not fiction or poetry, but more traditionally for a nineteenth-century woman, a book on household design, called *The Decoration of Houses*, written with Odgen Codman, the most fashionable architect of the day. Discarding the elaborate decoration of her mother's era, the stiff fussiness of Victorian America, Wharton simplifies the lines, disposes of the yards of fabric at the windows to allow light into the room, while at the same time arranging furniture and positioning doors to secure individual privacy and small group intimacy.

Spurred on by the achievement of her first book, Wharton went on to publish her first collection of short stories *The Greater Inclination*, in 1899. With her first book of fiction, her real identity began to form for her, even to "blossom" as she explains in her autobiography. The dis-eased and tentative "I" of her long years of early apprenticeship emerged from insignificance:

Any one walking along the streets might go into any bookshop, and say: "Please give me Edith Wharton's book", and the clerk, without bursting into incredulous laughter, would produce it, and be paid for it, and the purchaser would walk home with it and read it, and talk of it, and pass it on to other people to read! (*BG*, 113)

It is in her late thirties, an age when most traditional stories about women have ended, that Edith Wharton's story begins to take shape. Hers is not the story of romantic love, blissful marriage, plentiful children, rather hers is the story of literary work, social insight and prolific writing.

The short story volume was followed quickly by her first published novella *The Touchstone*, in 1900. Lucretia Jones fell into a coma that same year; after her death in 1901, the Whartons left Land's End, their home in Newport, Rhode Island, to settle in Lenox, Massachusetts, in the Berkshire Mountains, where they, or rather Edith, built the Mount, designing it on the architectural principles in her book on houses. At the Mount, Wharton could control her social obligations and, therefore, devote more of her time to her writing. As a final liberating gesture, she refused to sleep in the same room as Teddy, thus relieving her anxiety over his proximity.

In *The Decoration of Houses* Wharton argued that aesthetics embody values – character springs from houses, furnishings and decor. The Mount not only embodied her artistic taste but also expressed her desire for privacy and independence. Although she redecorated and restored numerous houses during her lifetime – apartments on Park Avenue in New York; Land's End in Newport, Rhode Island; apartments in the rue de Varenne in Paris; the Pavillon Colombe in St Brice-sous-forêt, a Parisian suburb; and Ste Claire in Hyères on the Mediterranean – the Berkshire house was the only one she built from scratch. It established a place for her in her late thirties and early forties to become a professional writer.

The Mount itself, patterned after Christopher Wren's Belton House, Lincolnshire, blended the private with the public world and symbolized Wharton's compromise between the two. The plan of the three-story house allows for limited socializing and considerable privacy. The grotto-like entrance hall at the back of the house on the

ground level restricts all but the favored few from a view
of the living quarters on the first floor, which look out
onto a private natural scene. A series of relatively small
rooms, connected by a long hallway, look out onto a stone
terrace, well-groomed formal gardens, Laurel Lake, and
the Berkshire Mountains. Teddy's den at one end of the
hall opens into Edith's library, a room twice as large. The
drawing room and dining room, though spacious, provide
room to accommodate small groups of friends; nowhere
does the plan allow space for the usual entertainment of
the New York/Newport social group the Whartons had
formerly belonged to – no room certainly for the 400 souls
in Mrs Astor's ballroom. The bedrooms on the second
floor suggest further privacy; Edith Wharton placed herself
in a separate wing, consisting of her bedroom, bath and
boudoir (which gave her a view of the entrance); this suite
could be closed off from the rest of the house. Although
connected to Teddy's room through a dressing room, it
is clear from the plan that she desired not company, but
solitude. In her study of Wharton, *Felicitous Space* (1986),
Judith Fryer begins with drawings, pictures, and a "tour"
of the Mount:

> What emerges most clearly from this plan is a sense
> of *order*: the careful symmetry allows for no unexpected
> mingling of servants and masters, no penetration of
> guests into private quarters, no romantic hermitages in
> the gardens, but rather a kind of social interaction that
> is carefully planned, controlled, deliberate.[7]

She quotes Henry James from *The American Scene* (1906),
where with his usual insight he describes the Mount as
containing *penetralia*, "some part ... sufficiently *within*
some other part, sufficiently withdrawn and consecrated,
not to constitute a thoroughfare." His vaginal, even womb-

like imagery, suggests the female nature of Wharton's house.

The Mount then gave Wharton a refuge from society, even from her husband, a place to "make up". She came to rely on her privacy there. Her house became her spiritual haven, sacred ground for the creation of her fiction. Over the course of her Lenox years (she often wrote as well in her Paris apartment), she completed an historical novel *The Valley of Decision (1902)*, another novella *Sanctuary* (1903), two books about Italian history and architecture *Italian Villas and Their Gardens* (1904) and *Italian Backgrounds* (1905), a best-seller about Old New York *The House of Mirth* (1905), a lesser known industrial novel *The Fruit of the Tree* (1907), an account of a trip she took with Henry James *A Motor-Flight Through France* (1908), a popular Hawthornesque tale about New England *Ethan Frome* (1911), her most Jamesian novel *The Reef* (1912), as well as many short stories, poems, two more novellas and a translation. The list of her work over the ten productive Lenox years reveals the steady pattern of her literary career; until the end of her life in 1937, she wrote, on average, a book or two every year, many of them best-sellers in their day and a significant number still widely read and studied.

At the Mount Edith Wharton began to move away from her insular, élite New York society toward an international, intellectual community of writers, scholars, historians, journalists, lawyers. It is fair to say, as Marilyn French has in her article "Muzzled Women", that Wharton never allowed her fictional heroines the freedom of movement she had in her own life.[8] She herself desired an escape from the restrictions placed on women, especially intellectual women, in Old New York society, and she was able to find that escape in her move to Paris where she attached herself to a new community of thinkers and writers. Most notable among them was Henry James, though critics have often overblown their relationship, especially in regard to his influence on her writing. She characterized their first meetings as her attempts to woo him as a woman might a lover. It's a curious way to tell the story of her entry into intellectual life unless we see it as another example of telling the socially-sanctioned tale of the adorned female in the world of men. She donned a "doucet" dress for their first encounter, a new hat for the second: as she self-mockingly explained, "[I]t would never have occurred to me that I had anything but my youth, and my pretty frock, to commend me" (*BG*, 172). R.W.B. Lewis notes that the two actually met in 1903. She was shy and distant, although James described her as "conversable", if "slightly cold".

Henry James's first letter to Edith Wharton had arrived in 1900, before their actual meeting. He responded to a short story she had sent him. "And I applaud, I mean I value, I egg you on in your study of the American life that surrounds you", James wrote in his characteristic style. "Let yourself go in it and *at* it – it's an untouched field, really: the folk who try, over there, don't come within miles of any civilized, however superficially, any 'evolved' life" (Lewis, 125). Two years later, in praising her efforts with her Italian historical novel *The Valley of Decision* (1902), James again urged her to "*Do New York!* The first-hand account is precious." He warned against his own "awful example of exile and ignorance" and expressed his desire "earnestly, tenderly, intelligently to admonish you, while you are young, free, expert, exposed ... admonish you, I say, in favour of the *American subject* (Lewis, 127)."[9]

Her initiation into intellectual friendships has always been told as a story about her contacts with men, her wooing of them and their influence on her. According to surviving letters, however, Edith Wharton's "awakening" to intellectual and literary life came in her contacts with

women as well as men. She began a correspondence with
Sara Norton, who had sent an admiring letter in 1899 after
the publication of *The Greater Inclination*. "I am so lacking
in self-confidence & my work falls so far short of what
I try for that I am almost childishly grateful for the least
word of approval."[10] Wharton responded in a self-effacing
tone she would use throughout her life about her work.
Over the long years of their friendship, she found with
Norton a camaraderie she never found with the many
prominent men who surrounded her. "It was so pleasant
to find", Wharton confessed in her 1901 letter to Norton,
"that we were *d'accord* on the more inaccessible subjects . . . that form either a barrier or a bridge to real friendship – such as I should like ours to be." She discovered
that bridge with few women, but it formed the basis of
her strong attachment to Sara Norton and later to another
intellectual, literary female friend, Margaret Terry
Chanler. She wrote to them as "Edith or Pussy as you
please" in the day when Sara was "Sally" and Margaret
was "Daisy". Using such "pet" names these women carried
on supportive, nurturing epistolary friendships that
centered on the quotidian world of homes, gardens, pets,
travel, friends, books and health.

From that record, a semi-private autobiographical story,
we see quite a different Edith Wharton than more public
accounts have drawn. We know from the letters to Norton
that the early days as a writer in Lenox were often lonely
ones. In May, 1901, for example, Wharton wrote to Norton
that it would be an act of philanthropy if she would visit:

> I seldom ask people to stay because I am obliged to
> lead such a quiet & systematic kind of life that the house
> is a dull one for visitors; but as you know Lenox &
> feel at home here I do not feel so shy about inviting
> you, especially as I think there are many things *we* enjoy
> talking of together. (*Letters*, 46)

Wharton made such overtures with the assurance that their similarities as isolated, intellectual females would draw them together.

In her response to an annual birthday letter (Norton always remembered her friend's January birthday), Wharton first made the obligatory complaint about middle age. "I excessively hate to be forty", she wrote. But then she discussed a more significant problem they both faced, not as middle-aged but as intellectual women:

> Don't I know that feeling you describe, when one longs to go to the hospital & *have something cut out*, & come out minus an organ, but alive & active & like other people, instead of dragging on with this bloodless exis-tence!! Only I fear you & I will never find a surgeon who will do us that service. (*Letters*, 55)

Certainly that sense of difference from other women struck intellectual women of their day. The "organ" that made them different, that made them literally and figuratively ill, was their intellect. Few scholars, however, have dwelled much on Wharton's kinship with women.

The more sensational story over the last ten years, since her letters and other personal papers have become known to the public, is the story of her sex life. Formerly, scholars believed her life to have been relatively sexless; the con-summation of her marriage had taken time and, many thought, soon excluded sex altogether: the Whartons never had children. R.W.B. Lewis and Cynthia Griffin Wolff, in their 1970s biographies of Wharton, discovered that the real passion of Wharton's life was directed not toward her husband nor, as earlier biographers had believed, toward her close personal friend Walter Berry but rather toward a journalist, Morton Fullerton, a man slightly younger than she, with considerably more sexual experience. Fullerton, a bisexual, philandering, mercurial lover, managed to

unearth considerable passion beneath Edith Wharton's
supposedly chilly surface. The strong-jawed, hawk-like,
corseted, fur-draped woman of letters had supposedly
belonged to the repressions of the nineteenth century;
ideologically conservative and emotionally aloof, she had
not before figured as an impulsive, sensual heroine.

The story of her passionate nature has come to light
in the publications of her letters to Fullerton by *The
Library Chronicle* (1985) and a much fuller selection of
her correspondence by R.W.B. and Nancy Lewis, *The Letters of Edith Wharton* (1988). Here is a story, embedded
in the love letters she wrote Fullerton and he refused to
destroy, that everyone understands, a version of the Sleeping Beauty: a nearly lifeless woman awakened by the
embrace of a fiery young man. In the Fullerton correspondence, she becomes a woman in the flesh:

> And if you can't come into the room without my feeling
> all over me a ripple of flame, & if, wherever you touch
> me, a heart beats under your touch, & if, when you
> hold me, & I don't speak, it's because all the words
> in me seem to have become throbbing pulses, & all my
> thoughts are a great golden blur – why should I be afraid
> of your smiling at me, when I can turn the beads &
> calico back into such beauty – ? (*Letters* 135)

What we have learned from her letters is that though she
may have repressed emotion earlier in her life, she was
by her mid-forties a fully passionate, extraordinarily articulate woman.

We also learn that scholars and readers continue to
prefer the conventional story of female success and happiness. If Edith Wharton's marriage was a very incomplete
affair, then perhaps her sexual liaison with Fullerton provided the plot every woman is supposed to desire. Wolff,

in her psychobiography *A Feast of Words: The Triumph of Edith Wharton* (1977), finds in Wharton's life a familiar female text: Wharton's sexual awakening with Fullerton triggered not only her emotional maturing, but also the maturing of her fiction.

Following her lead, Sandra Gilbert and Susan Gubar in their massive feminist revision of modernism, *No Man's Land* (1989), have written elegantly on Wharton's life and her fiction, but end by focusing on the remnants of erotica left from her life: the love letters to Fullerton, a love diary of her "Life Apart" with him, some love poetry and a pornographic fragment, "Beatrice Palmato", detailing the sexual coupling of a father and daughter. For them the last test of "utopian feminism" is a woman's ability to articulate the "unsayable" or "what is erotically illicit", and Wharton has passed the test through her "concealed commitment to the subversive credo of erotic self-possession" (164). They are right to argue that Edith Wharton came to possess herself, although they reduce her achievement to eroticism as though that were the final way of marking female success. Wharton's self-possession, although it included her abandonment of traditional notions of marriage and sexual fidelity, went beyond the erotic. The truth is that Wharton came to possess herself, not through the brief passion of an affair in her forties, but through her steady passion for writing and for ordering her own life.

The affair with Fullerton, which probably lasted three or four years, accompanied the breakdown of the Wharton marriage. Teddy himself had turned to other women, supposedly housing them at his wife's expense. Letters and various accounts show that as Edith Wharton gained recognition as a writer and an intellectual, she found a robust emotional health, while her husband Teddy became depressed, anxious, eventually mentally ill. The Whartons, after many disagreements and trials, finally separated and divorced. What is significant to her story as a writer is that amid the weary agitated years of their waning marriage and the emotional shifts in her affair with Morton Fullerton, Edith Wharton continued her morning routine of writing. In spite of personal rupture and intense disappointment, she wrote book after book. By the time of her divorce in 1913, she had become, according to many critics and scholars, perhaps the best American writer of her time.

In her fifties, divorced from her husband, abandoned by her lover, scorned by her social group, Edith Wharton would seem to have excluded herself from any possible female success story. And yet, quite the opposite is true. We might argue, in fact, that the story of the rest of her life is such a satisfying one precisely because all the men around her failed to provide her a more traditional life.

Teddy's breakdown made a longer marriage impossible; Morton Fullerton's philandering ensured the relatively short duration of their affair and the unsuitability of a marriage to him; and Walter Berry's reticence with women proved the basis of a lifelong friendship without marriage. In her selection of men, Edith Wharton, as it turns out, chose wisely. The survival of her marriage or, certainly, any subsequent remarriage would have taken time and energy away from the independent, creative, fulfilling life she fashioned for herself in late middle age. This is precisely the time in a woman's life, Carolyn Heilbrun argues, that offers the most original text: "It is perhaps only in old age, certainly past fifty, that women can stop being female impersonators, can grasp the opportunity to reverse their most cherished principles of 'femininity'" (*Writing a Woman's Life*, 126). Wharton had passed the age of conventional romance, marriage, motherhood, the usual narratives that give shape to a woman's life and promise her eventual happiness. What she had in late middle age were talent, health, independence, a plentiful and secure income, a group of supportive friends, both male and female.

Her first move was to leave New York, indeed leave America, to resettle herself in France; she spent her last twenty-five years as an expatriate writer, returning to her own country only once in 1923, to receive an honorary degree from Yale University, the first such honor given to a woman by a major American university. In Paris, she lived in the rue de Varenne, a quiet, exclusive street on the Left Bank. Here she found a stable culture, rich in history, full of the accumulations of values and rituals she believed promoted the best in human nature. As Shari Benstock, in *Women of the Left Bank: Paris, 1900–1940* (1986), points out, Wharton settled herself into "the most conservative of drawing rooms", in the Faubourg St Germain where she discovered that "Paris could offer independence without the accompanying penalty of isolation."[11] That is to say, in Paris Wharton found a comfortable compromise: she could be an intellectual, literary woman and still belong to and be respected by a community she admired.

She had little more than settled herself when Germany threatened to destroy the very people, buildings, art, culture she admired. During the years of the First World War, Edith Wharton went into battle with the same enthusiasm, the same energy she used in organizing her own life. In 1914, at the very outbreak of the fighting, she started a workroom for seamstresses; later in the year, she began the American Hostels for Refugees to provide shelter for homeless victims of the war; in 1915, she organized the Children of Flanders Rescue Committee. She founded, organized, and ran her relief programs as any able, talented, energetic administrator would. By the end of the first year alone, she reported that her hostel had assisted hundreds of people by providing meals, medical care and jobs. In 1916, she planned and edited *The Book*

of the Homeless, a collection of essays, stories, poems,
sketches, even pieces of music donated by distinguished
contemporaries, providing $15,000 to the rescue effort.
In letters and articles she pleaded with her Old New York
friends for money as well.

Her account of the progress of the war *Fighting France
from Dunkerque to Belport* (1915), began as a series of
articles she had written for *Scribner's*. It became part of
a series of books reporting on the war. The volume
on England, written by Wharton's friend Mary [Mrs
Humphry] Ward begins with the picture of a British battle-
ship, the volume on Eastern Europe with a sketch of a
slavic soldier, the one on Italy with a picture of the King
of Italy and the Prince of Wales, and the one on the early
battles in the trenches with a portrait of the King of
Belgium.

Wharton chose however to begin with a picture of *herself*
at the front, subtitled "A French Palisade". She celebrated
her own involvement in the fighting, the first-hand view
she had of the war; supposedly she was the first woman
to see the front lines at Verdun. Her patriotic, even jingois-
tic, fervor sounds in her two novels about the war, *The
Marne* (1918) and *A Son at the Front* (1923), both stories
about traditional manly heroism in battle. To instruct
Americans in French culture, she wrote another series of
articles about French society and its difference from and
superiority to American society; the essays were collected
into *French Ways and Their Meaning* (1919).[12] In that book
about French culture, Wharton used her reading of French
society to illustrate her own cultural ideals. For her intense
francophilia, particularly in the form of her war effort,
the French made her a chevalier of the French Legion
of Honor.

And it is here, essentially, in *A Backward Glance* that
she stopped telling her story, or very much of it. It is also
here, in her sixties, that scholars and critics have, in a

sense, left her, as well. Supposedly, the final years follow a pattern of steady decline in her work and in her personal life. Yet during these years, she was as productive and popular a writer as she ever was. Throughout the 1920s, however, Wharton had the increasing sense that her fiction was being misread. Writing to Margaret Chanler after the critics misunderstood the ending of her novel *The Mother's Recompense* (1925), Wharton measured the distance between her intention and her critics' interpretation:

> You will wonder that the priestess of the Life of Reason shd take such things to heart; & I wonder too. I never have minded before; but as my work reaches its close, I feel so sure that it is either nothing, or far more than they know . . . And I wonder, a little desolately, which? (*Letters*, 483)

Many readers and critics believed that she had adapted her style to fit the slick magazines of the 1920s; increasingly distant from the New York of her youth and middle age, many argued that she either borrowed depictions of modern America or reverted nostalgically to an idealized view of her past. They were right, I think, to notice the change in her writing after the war, but the wholesale dismissal of her later works is more the result of a failure to read the novels, rather than their inferior quality. It is fair to say that the later novels are not the work of a rigorous social historian, as her earlier novels had been, but rather they dwell more on the psychology of the individual member of society. Not unlike other modernist works of the period, she sought a psychologically rich portrait of the stresses on the individual in the ceaselessly moving culture of the anxious twenties, a world she likened to an escalator, ever flowing but tending nowhere. In such a world of paradoxical flux and stasis, she depicted the search of the individual for safe, fixed ground.

The critic's story of her waning career, of the inability
of age to produce agile, inventive, strong-minded fiction
fits a conventional tale. Her steady, successful work over
the last fifteen years of her life belies that standard story
of age and decline. *The Age of Innocence* began a productive period of writing, including *The Glimpses of the
Moon* (1922), *A Son at the Front* (1923), *Old New York*
(1924), *The Mother's Recompense* and *The Writing of Fiction* (both in 1925), *Twilight Sleep* (1927), *The Children*
(1928), *Hudson River Bracketed* (1929) and its sequel *The
Gods Arrive* (1932), *A Backward Glance* (1934), along with
many short stories, including several ghost stories, and the
posthumously published novel *The Buccaneers* (1938).
Most of her novels were best-sellers in their day, although
they have since declined. Two of her novels, *The Mother's
Recompense* and *The Children*, are currently being re-
evaluated upwards and others, especially *Twilight Sleep*,
Hudson River Bracketed and its sequel *The Gods Arrive*,
are being reconsidered.

When we look again at the later third of her life, we
can see the story as a love story of a very different sort
than we are used to telling about women and certainly
a different story from the one told about her early life.
It is a love story, not about a woman and her husband
or about a woman and her lover, but a love story of an
altogether different sort, one rarely told. Wharton's first
love was her house, the structure that allowed her to order
her life, giving the mornings to her art and the afternoons
to society. After the war, Wharton settled herself into two
houses, one she called the Pavillon Colombe, a former
home of courtesans in St Brice-sous-forêt, just north of
Paris, and the other Ste Claire, a former nunnery, nearly
destroyed by German attacks during the war, situated in
Hyères on the Mediterranean. The juxtaposition of cour-
tesan and nun, the irony of such a marriage, must have
pleased Wharton as she shuttled from one to the other,

as Gilbert and Gubar have noted, in a female world. Like the Mount, these houses provided solitude, a silence in which to write.

If we retell the story of Edith Wharton's life without placing romance and marriage at the center, if we allow her art that central position, then we can tell a very different story. The point is not that her marriage to Teddy Wharton failed, or that her lover Morton Fullerton abandoned her, or even that her closest male friend Walter Berry never proposed. Instead we can tell a story about Edith Wharton's career, especially about her finding a house, a room, a place to write. We find the details of that story, interestingly, not in public accounts of her life, but in private ones, in her letters to her friends.

"I am thrilled to the spine," she wrote to Royall Tyler in 1919 as she prepared to move into Ste Claire, "I feel as if I were going to get married – to the right man at last!" (*Letters*, 417). And the "marriage" suited her well; she spent the warm months in St Brice and the cool ones in Hyères, where she could write, garden, entertain, coordinate and command her material and fictive worlds. As she moved into Ste Claire for Christmas of 1920, she wrote to her sister-in-law Mary Cadwalader "Minnie" Jones, "[Y]esterday was the happiest Xmas I have spent in many a long year. I can wish no old woman of my age a better one!" (*Letters*, 436). The house has all the characteristics of a satisfying lover, "delicious", "friendly", "comfortable". As she explains her life to Minnie, she points out, "It is good to grow old – as well as to die – 'in beauty'; & the beauty of this little place is inexhaustible." Edith Wharton found in Hyères the same environment she had built earlier in Lenox. As she put it to her friend Bernard Berenson, "It's only at Hyères that I own myself" (*Letters*, 453). From such a perch, the hawklike eye created the "significant *I*", the fiction "worthy of preservation".

2 Edith Wharton's Fiction

But what does "human nature" ... consist in, and how much of it is left when it is separated from the web of customs, manners, culture it has elaborately spun about itself?

– Edith Wharton, "The Great American Novel"

To a torn heart uncomforted by human nearness a room may open almost human arms, and the being to whom no four walls mean more than any others, is, at such hours, expatriate everywhere.

– Edith Wharton, *The House of Mirth*

Edith Wharton once quarreled with William Dean Howells over the relationship of the self to society. Henry James, so the story goes, complained to Howells about the scarcity of materials for the novelist in America's rudimentary social order, an argument that stretches back to James Fenimore Cooper who likewise argued that it would "baffle the strength of a giant" to find social material for a novel of manners about American culture. Howells responded to James that beyond the social order, "There is the whole of human nature!" That is to say, Howells separated the "self" from "society" and argued that the essence of selfhood lay outside social boundaries.

Responding to Howells, Wharton asked in her essay "The Great American Novel":

> But what does "human nature" thus denuded consist in, and how much of it is left when it is separated from the web of customs, manners, culture it has elaborately spun about itself? Only that hollow unreality, "Man," an evocation of the eighteenth-century demagogues who were the first inventors of "standardization." As to real men, unequal, unmanageable, and unlike each other, they are all bound up with the effects of climate, soil, laws, religion, wealth – and, above all, leisure.[1]

Identity for Wharton is inextricably bound to culture, to one's material and social environment. "Traditional society," she argues in the same essay, "with its old established distinctions of class, its pass–words, exclusions, delicate shades of language and behavior, is one of man's oldest works of art, the least conscious and the most instinctive." She might have said "one of woman's oldest works of art", in that women have traditionally been seen as the creators and guardians of the social world, especially in American culture.

The bond between the individual and the social group, "the web of customs, manners, culture", lies at the heart of Edith Wharton's fiction. Her novels and short stories depict individuals enmeshed in what she metaphorically called the social "web" or "net", an elaborate weave of manners, mores, rituals, expectations, gestures as well as physical environment, houses, streets, rooms, decor, costume that define the parameters of human experience, even human nature. As she knew from her own experience as a woman in Old New York, society is a "hieroglyphic world", a coded world of signs that individuals must learn to read and interpret in order to make the personal adjustments, however difficult, between individual desire and

social necessity. Human nature, for her, was clothed in
the social fabric; she saw no possibility for life denuded
of that garment, no essential "human nature" outside the
elaborately woven social context. The story she had to
tell in her fiction delineated the dialectic features of the
social bond: the bonds or restrictions society places on
the individual and the resulting bond or covenant between
the two.[2]

In the traditional literary canon, the American quest
has most often been depicted as a male journey away from
the domestic, social world of women toward the open road.
The male story, especially as it has developed in American
literature, follows a route perhaps best outlined by Ralph
Waldo Emerson in his essay "Self-Reliance" (1839):

> Society everywhere is in conspiracy against the manhood
> of every one of its members. Society is a joint-stock
> company, in which the members agree for the better
> securing of his bread to each shareholder, to surrender
> the liberty and culture of the eater. The virtue in most
> request is conformity. Self-reliance is its aversion. ...
> Whoso would be a man, must be a nonconformist.

Emerson's references to his audience, "manhood" and
"man", heighten the essential maleness of his argument;
man is caught in a struggle to free himself from the restrictions of society; indeed, a man can mature only by severing
that tie. Emerson's popularizing of the revolutionary ideals
of the eighteenth century, especially his articulation of the
ideal of autonomous selfhood, has become the touchstone
of American literature.

The hero of Nathaniel Hawthorne's tale "Young Goodman Brown" (1835) is the model for the American man
who must leave home to find himself. As he journeys off
down the road at sunset, he turns to get a last look at

Faith, the wife he leaves behind: "Well, she's a blessed angel on earth; and after this one night I'll cling to her skirts and follow her to heaven." His manhood, even his identity, is tested away from home. And, other writers, following Hawthorne's lead, have sent their heroes on similar quests. Ishmael, for example, in Herman Melville's *Moby Dick* (1851) finds that the only antidote to depression is to take to the sea: "If they but knew it, almost all men in their degree, some time or other, cherish very nearly the same feelings towards the ocean with me." And later, Mark Twain's Huck Finn sounds the same note even at the very end of his journey on the raft: "But I reckon I got to light out for the Territory ahead of the rest, because Aunt Sally she's going to adopt me and sivilize me and I can't stand it. I been there before." In that story of American experience the female is associated with society, which threatens manhood; the male quest is to escape the stifling force of female "sivilization."

D. H. Lawrence, in his *Studies in Classic American Literature* (1923), viewed the American tale as the story of a national escape from the civilizing forces of Europe – a mark of social immaturity. Lawrence Buell, in a recent essay. "American Pastoral Ideology Reappraised" (1989), argues that to overcome our parochial view of American literary studies, we must learn to see its similarity to other postcolonial cultures and literatures; he agrees, in a sense, with Lawrence that the pastoral romance is rooted in colonial experience. Leslie Fiedler in *Love and Death in the American Novel* (1960) couched the phenomenon in more personal terms by characterizing American literature as the story of man on the run. In that configuration, man versus society, the thoroughly American story details the journey of the hero away from society, essentially from adult responsibility. That is to say, both models posit escape from society as an immature impulse, marking the desire to avoid more complex social structures. In its telling the American story has become implicitly and explicitly a male quest, providing an environment for masculine adventure outside the domestic setting, where presumably the women rule.

What happens when the protagonist is a woman? Where is she to go? What territory might she, in Huck Finn's phrase, "light out" for? If autonomous selfhood has become the ideal model for American literature, how can women in the conventional workings of society become heroic? Few women have been whalers or riverboat pilots. The open road has never held the same promise for women as it has for men. The woman's story has taken place, for the most part, in the home and in society, the realm of the relational, not the autonomous self. The woman's story has traditionally placed both male and female protagonists within society, the community is in essence the "territory". Edith Wharton's fiction, like that of other American women writers, tells the story of the self within society.

If we look at the canon of American literature through the lens of female, rather than male experience, we see a dramatically different picture. Striking at the heart of a literary canon that had by the mild-twentieth century crystallized into a nearly all-male cast,[3] feminist critics of American literature, especially Annette Kolodny in *The Lay of the Land* (1975) and *The Land Before Her* (1984) and Nina Baym in *Woman's Fiction* (1978), have attacked the centrality of the male romance to the American experience. If we place Eve as well as Adam in the Edenic wilderness, we see, in Kolodny's words, that Eve hoped "a raw frontier might yet sustain viable images of home." That is to say, the female dream for the new land has not been to escape from society, but rather to build a new one in the wilderness. The female story has emphasized a different configuration: not man *versus* society, but rather man and woman *within* society. It is precisely the female

configuration, individuals within the social structure, that
forms the core of Wharton's fiction.

Feminist revisions of Freudian psychological development may help us to see this tension between female and
male stories in a clearer light. In *The Reproduction of
Mothering* (1978) Nancy Chodorow argues that previous
theories of human psychology have placed the male at the
center, as the norm for maturation at each developmental
stage. Overlooked, for the most part, is the fact that children, both male and female, have traditionally had their
primary relationship with a woman, the mother who gives
birth to them and does most of the rearing as well. That
imbalance in the relationship between parents and children
may account for the very different ways male and female
children seek their identity. In that system the male child
must develop those traits that set him apart from the
mother; autonomous selfhood fits that cultural division.
Maleness or manhood opposes female norms and beha-
viors. To mature the male must move away from the largely
female world around him. The female, to the contrary,
must identify with the mother in order to develop her sexual and psychological sense of self. She stays with the
mother, using that notion of femininity as her norm, repro-
ducing the mothering she has known. Chodorow uses this
model to account for the relational quality of female interaction:

From very early, then, because they are parented by
a person of the same gender (a person who has already
internalized a set of unconscious meanings, fantasies,
and self-images about this gender and brings to her
experience her own internalized early relationship to her
own mother), girls come to experience themselves as
less differentiated than boys, as more continuous with
and related to the external object-world and as differently oriented to their inner object-world as well.[4]

To posit, as earlier psychoanalytic theory did, that the male represents the model for maturation, left the female outside the process.

Following Chodorow, Carol Gilligan in her study of female psychological development, *In a Different Voice* (1982), finds that women's stories likewise differ from men's:

> In their portrayal of relationships, women replace the bias of men toward separation with a representation of the interdependence of self and other, both in love and in work. By changing the lens of developmental observation from individual achievement to relationships of care, women depict ongoing attachment as the path that leads to maturity.[5]

Using this model, we can expect that the man's story will feature autonomous selfhood as the path to maturity and the woman's story will gather relational selfhood as the center of the mature life.

Especially in American society, where during the nineteenth century men and women divided sharply between socially imposed gender roles, the man in the public and the woman in the private sphere, we would expect Chodorow's and Gilligan's theories to make sense. Unlike male versions of the western adventure, female mythology produced domestic stories that end in community not endless individuality. American women writers in the nineteenth century told the woman's story – a tale of social interaction and domesticity – with a financial success much greater than that of their male contemporaries, who dubbed them, in Hawthorne's words, "the damned mob of scribbling women". Writers like Susan Warner, E.D.E.N. Southworth, Louisa May Alcott, and Elizabeth Stuart Phelps wrote novels that comfortably situated the heroine in a world of marriage and motherhood. The female domestic story has been regarded, during and since that time, by male writers, critics and readers as a merely "popular" genre, a type of female romance which presents ideal domesticity and avoids its threat to the individual. The same critics, as I have discussed, have judged the male romance, the pastoral adventure away from society, to be the genre of "serious" literature.

Much like her contemporary female American writers, especially Kate Chopin in *The Awakening* (1899), Willa Cather in *The Professor's House* (1925), or Ellen Glasgow in *Barren Ground* (1925), Edith Wharton sought to correct the errors of both the female domestic novel and the male pastoral romance. The social bond is made up of two opposing forces, the bond that restricts the individual and the one that unites them in common effort. Unlike novelists who celebrated domesticity, Wharton presented the bonds or restrictions imposed on the individual; and unlike romancers who celebrated escape, she depicted the inevitable bond or covenant between the two and the impossibility of getting beyond the community.

Her fictive world is peopled with both men and women, who must struggle for selfhood within the social context; she insistently and, many critics have claimed, even perversely avoids the easy, happy ending. In *French Ways and Their Meaning* (1919), where so much of Wharton's philosophy is exposed, she used another anecdote about Howells to explain the conflict between her own view of the world and that held by her audience. The two writers once discussed "the strange exigency of the American public which compels the dramatist (if he wishes to be played) to wind up his play, whatever its point of departure, with the 'happily-ever-after' of the fairy-tales." As Wharton put it, Americans "want to be harrowed (and even slightly shocked) from eight until ten-thirty, and then consoled and reassured before eleven" (65). That tale is appropriate, she argued, to the land of the nursery, where the

audience is clearly immature and therefore in need of shelter from the harsh reality of adult living. But grownups,
Wharton believed, needed a healthy dose of the truth
about reality:

> Things are not always and everywhere well with the
> world, and each man has to find it out as he grows up.
> It is the finding out that makes him grow, and until he
> has faced the fact and digested the lesson he is not grown
> up – he is still in the nursery. (66)

People need a "violent and tragic awakening" she insisted,
and her fiction awakens characters and readers alike to
the often grim possibilities of socially engaged living. The
point for Wharton was not that life is too difficult to be
borne, but that mature individuals see the "adventure"
for what it is, full of imperfections and entanglements.

Her novels – especially *The House of Mirth, The Fruit
of the Tree, Ethan Frome, Summer* and *The Age of Innocence* – stress the bonds put upon the individual by the
social group. Protagonists from Lily Bart to Newland
Archer must learn the coded meanings and values of their
culture in order to exert any control over their destinies
and, in spite of their attempts, they are more often blind-
sided by messages they are unable or unwilling to read
and interpret clearly. Yet in each case the protagonist
measures individual bondage against social bonding and,
in the end, adheres to the social covenant.

Her heroes and heroines all struggle to find an accep-
table, secure place within their social order; they seek a
metaphorical and often literal home in order to define their
sense of self. For example in *The House of Mirth*, her
first novel about American society, finding a house or home
is a dominant theme. Many of the minor characters have
a house: the wealthy Trenors live amid the luxury and
elegance of their sumptuous mansion Bellomont; Gerty

Farish, the model of the new independent *fin-de-siècle* woman, has also found a home, albeit a "dingy" flat; and even the poor, working-class Struther family has through hard work earned a meager but clean flat, a nest hanging "safely over the abyss". Those who have secured a place within society have reached, the heroine Lily Bart (who ironically never finds comfortable quarters) concludes, "the central truth of existence" (*HM*, 319). Wharton's narrator explains the importance of one's physical place: "To a torn heart uncomforted by human nearness a room may open almost human arms, and the being to whom no four walls mean more than any others, is, at such hours, expatriate everywhere" (*HM*, 148).

"Expatriate everywhere" is perhaps the most frightening fate for a Wharton character. Those who begin outside society seek ways in, even hire social savants to school them in the manners, nuances, skills required to blend into the larger community. Simon Rosedale and Undine Spragg, both on Horatio-Alger-like climbs through the labyrinths of money and power, enlist the knowledge of those who understand the meaning of the social "hieroglyphics" they must learn to read – people like Carrie Fisher and Lily Bart in *The House of Mirth* or even Mrs Heeney, the masseuse in the more bitingly satirical novel *The Custom of the Country*.

Yet Wharton does not tell the story of those who seek and find, rather her intensely ironic novels focus on the lives of the malcontents, those somehow at odds with the larger community. Her protagonists all rebel against the place allotted them by fate: Lily Bart refuses to marry money in order to secure a stable place in New York society; Ethan Frome longs to escape the ramshackle house bequeathed to him by his parents; Charity Royall makes a temporary home for herself in the Berkshire woods rather than accept without struggle the house offered by her stepfather; Newland Archer hopes to abandon both house and wife in New York to flee to an imaginary world with Ellen Olenska; even Wharton's cruelly successful protagonist Undine Spragg continually looks for ever more sumptuous quarters.

In this desire for escape, Wharton's heroes and heroines echo the lament of the heroes of male romance – Goodman Brown, Ishmael, Huck Finn. Yet to be "expatriate everywhere" is to lose one's sense of self. In Edith Wharton's fiction to get beyond society, metaphorically and even literally to get out of the house, is to annihilate the self. The open road may lure Wharton's protagonists, but they soon find that the only territory finally open to them is the community; to survive they must, like Justine Brent in *The Fruit of the Tree* (1907), learn that life is "a succession of pitiful compromises with fate, of concessions to old traditions, old beliefs, old charities and frailties" (*FT*, 624).

Like the scientific thinkers of her day, a group of writers she read and admired, Wharton thought of survival in terms of fitness. Her version of that popularized phrase "survival of fittest", however, significantly revised its meaning. In her fiction the survivors are not the physically strongest or "fittest" characters, not even necessarily the economically strongest ones, but rather those who best "fit" their social and economic place. The conflict in her fiction does not so much feature battles between foes for place, although sometimes characters do engage in social combat, rather the main conflict is between personal desire and social necessity, the winner being the one who is best able to conform or "fit" the intricately patterned, enormously powerful social structure. Successful characters have secured a social, even a physical space in their world. That space may be as impressive as the Trenor mansion or as meager as the Struther flat. Both represent nests over the abyss of alienation or perpetual expatriation. Characters who "fit" have space to live; those who fail to "fit" – because of psychological temperament or social background or economic conditions – have no space to survive, are indeed doomed.

Like protagonists in the naturalist or determinist novels of her day, Wharton's heroes and heroines are figuratively "manacled" to their fate, beyond rescue. In her essay "Confessions of a Novelist", Wharton responded to her critics who often accused her of unwarranted cruelty in her failure to mitigate the fates of her characters:

> It is necessary to me that the note of inevitableness should be sounded at the very opening of my tale, and that my characters should go forward to their ineluctable doom. . . . From the first I know exactly what is going to happen to every one of them; their fate is settled beyond rescue, and I have but to watch and record.[6]

We can hear in the insistence of her tone, Edith Wharton's determination to rewrite the American story of limitless opportunity and inevitable success, the fixation of American ideology on "liberty and justice" and "the pursuit of happiness". What if, she posits, the social world is oppressive *and* the individual cannot escape?

We can also hear in the cool objectivity of her stance, Wharton's desire to appear neutral, distant, outside the picture she is painting.[7] That feature of her writing, a quasi-scientific pose, has always invited criticism from readers, friends and critics alike. In order to tell the story of the individual within society and to tell it without the sentimentality of female domestic novelists, Wharton sought and borrowed the "objective" tone and jargon of the male scientific discourse of her day.

Edith Wharton wrote to Sara Norton in 1907 that there was no literary genre she enjoyed better than scientific books. She read several current scientific texts from 1907, including: Gustave le Bon's *L'Evolution des forces*,

Charles Jean Julien Deperet's *Les transformations du monde animal*, Vernon Kellogg's *Darwinism Today*, and Robert Lock's *Recent Progress in the Study of Variation, Heredity, and Evolution (Letters*, 135, 145 & 151). She claimed that Darwin, Spencer, Lecky and Taine had been the formative intellectual influences of her youth. Wharton's reading of *The Origin of Species* (1859) when she was twenty-two provided her with the most exciting intellectual experience of her life. Steeping herself in such male scientific discourse, she found a literary stance, a perspective from which to view the social drama surrounding her. What she saw in such theories about the shaping force of biology and especially environment was a substantiation of her own view, one she knew first-hand from the social, economic and political world of Old New York. Her adoption of male models of scientific, sociological, anthropological investigation gave her voice, a female and therefore culturally less powerful one, the ring of male authority.

She drew stark portraits of extraordinary figures who struggle to coexist with the intricately woven culture around them. Few of her protagonists are able to mount more than a futile attack against the corruptions, the distortions, the coercions of their society. They all echo Charity Royall's lament in the novel *Summer*: "In the established order of things as she knew them she saw no place for her individual adventure" (*S*, 174). The order of things at odds with the desire for individual adventure lies at the heart of most American fiction, but Wharton differs from many of her compatriot writers in that she denies her characters romantic, illusory, or idealistic escape. There is no open road in her tales, or rather the supposed route away curves and loops back to the community. Survival for her characters depends on their ability to compromise, to find a way to "fit" into the larger, more powerful community. Such a philosophy, forced on her characters by thwarted desire, may lead, Wharton suggests, to real maturity. The struggle, all along, takes place within the social arena; in Wharton's world there is, as many critics have noted, no exit from the group and its traditions, beliefs, charities and frailties.

Her determinist point of view links her to Zola and the Goncourts in France, Hardy in England, and certain American writers of her day, Theodore Dreiser, Frank Norris, and Stephen Crane. She spurned the so-called "naturalist" movement in literature, the doctrine developed and popularized by Zola, who announced in his essay "The Experimental Novel" (1880) that the experimental or scientific method could be applied to literature. He set out to demonstrate in his own fiction that the scientific method could be used to gather knowledge about human passion and intellect: "The problem is to learn what such and such a passion, acting in such and such a milieu under such and such circumstances, will bring about in terms of the individual and of society."[8] Wharton read and enjoyed his novels but deplored his programmatic rhetoric. What she found, however, was that in her study of the interrelationship between the social group and the individual member certain conditions – cultural, economic, geographical, climatic and at times biological – exert great force over human will.

She traced her own philosophical determinism through male European intellectual thought that fixes the individual in a social, cultural, historical context as opposed to the romantic selfhood of American colonial thought that places the individual outside society. Hippolyte Taine, who in his famous introduction to the *History of English Literature* (1863) argued that literature itself is the product of *race, milieu* and *moment*, especially won her respect. For him the novel had become the scientific study of the effects of these factors on character. "Whether the data are physical or moral makes no difference"; he claimed, "they always have causes; there are causes for ambition, courage, truthfulness, just as there are for digestion, muscular movement, or animal heat."[9] Houses, streets, furniture, costume, no less than habits, tastes, refinements, make up the individual: "All these externals are so many avenues converging to one centre, and you follow these only to reach that centre; here is the real man, namely, that group of faculties and of sentiments which produces the rest." It is difficult to find a philosophy closer to Wharton's own.

As one would expect, naturalist clichés creep into Wharton's writing. In *The House of Mirth*, for example, Lily Bart, who seems to have absorbed the rhetoric of the naturalists, tells Lawrence Selden, "I was just a screw or cog in the great machine I called life" (*HM*, 308). Ethan Frome, although he could not articulate his situation, found that, "The inexorable facts closed in on him like prison-warders handcuffing a convict. There was no way out – none" (*EF*, 134). In her industrial novel *The Fruit of the Tree*, Wharton presents the town of Hanaford as a villainous force: "In obedience to the grim law of industrial prosperity, it would soon lose its one lingering grace and spread out in unmitigated ugliness, devouring green fields and shaded slopes like some insect plague consuming the land" (*FT*, 24). Much later, in *The Age of Innocence* Wharton adopts the language of the anthropologist. As Ellen Olenska is ousted from the New York clan, Wharton tells us, "There were certain things that had to be done, and if done at all, done handsomely and thoroughly: and one of these, in the New York code, was the tribal rally around a kinswoman about to be eliminated from the tribe" (*AI*, 334). As Archer begins to understand the forces of tradition and training, he feels "like a prisoner in the center of an armed camp" (*AI*, 335). In such widely differing novels, Wharton makes the same point: human nature is inseparable from "the web of customs, manners, culture" spun about it. Her characters, all caught in the "machine" or "prison" or "code" or "web", are restricted by the bond.

Wharton traced her literary tradition through a group of equally tough-minded realists: Austen, Eliot, and Thackeray in England, Balzac and Flaubert in France, and Tolstoy in Russia. In *The Writing of Fiction* (1924), Wharton argued that Balzac was the first writer "to see his people, physically and morally, in their habit as they lived, with all their personal hobbies and infirmities" (*WF*, 5). What she most admired was his ability "to draw this dramatic action as much from the relation of his characters to their houses, streets, towns, professions, inherited habits and opinions, as from their fortuitous contacts with each other." Here Wharton finds in Balzac her own method of literary presentation.

She might have simply stated her own literary technique, her own philosophical bent; instead she directed attention away from herself, explaining the work of Balzac rather than her own. In that sense *The Writing of Fiction*, her literary autobiography, does the same thing her personal autobiography *A Backward Glance*, would later do. Both narratives move away from her story, outward toward the lives, talents and literary work of others, especially men. The decidedly male direction of her philosophical and literary eduction allowed her to link herself, as she had earlier walked at her father's side, to the dominant culture, the intellectual and public world of the powerful white male. Supposedly "objective" scientific discourse gave her female voice the power of male rhetoric.

To go beyond the web of social relationships, entanglements, rituals, expectations and values is essentially to annihilate the self. Wharton makes that point in novel after novel. Her protagonists, both female and male, begin with a sense of Emerson's autonomous selfhood; they see that society is, in some way, in a conspiracy against their individuality, their desire to control their social fate. Yet when

they "light out" for some new territory beyond their
immediate social world, Wharton turns them back, catches
them inextricably in the social web.

The passion of rebellion springs up in Wharton's protagonists, who long to free themselves from social restrictions. To get beyond convention becomes their dream.
For instance, Lily Bart's emblem in *The House of Mirth*
is a seal with "Beyond! beneath a flying ship": it symbolizes
her desire to follow Lawrence Selden's Emersonian course
away from social obligations into "a republic of the spirit".
At twenty-nine, Lily is under the social imperative to marry
soon, and to marry well. Yet the wealthy men at her disposal are self-absorbed and, to her mind, dull. Percy
Gryce, whose real passion is collecting Americana, might
offer her marriage in return for the privilege of boring
her for life. Instead Lily wanders with Selden in the woods,
a usual stage for the American romantic adventure; there
he offers her his "republic" as a refuge from her social
dilemma:

> "My idea of success," he said, "is personal free-
> dom."
> "Freedom? Freedom from worries?" [Lily asked.]
> "From everything – from money, from poverty,
> from ease and anxiety, from all the material accidents.
> To keep a kind of republic of the spirit – that's what
> I call a success." (*HM*, 68)

That is to say, Lawrence Selden offers Lily Bart a male
myth of success, an escape from the demands of society.
But Lily, as a woman, cannot get beyond. Without marrying a wealthy man or inheriting money, she falls prey to
poverty, illness, depression, eventually drugs and death.
To fall, as she does, outside "the web of customs, manners,
culture" of her initial social group, is to annihilate her
individual self.

Edith Wharton's stories follow this theme and its variation. In the satiric portrait of female success, *The Custom of the Country*, the would-be heroine Undine Spragg represents the reverse of Lily Bart. She rises in New York and European societies by using marriage, first to a hometown Apex boy, then an Old New York aristocrat, and later a French nobleman, and finally to the same Apex man, who over the course of the novel has become a financial success on Wall Street. Ironically, Wharton also uses "beyond" as Undine's motto: "There was something still better beyond, then – more luxurious, more exciting, more worthy of her!" (*CC*, 54). Yet marry and divorce as she might, there is no way to get beyond for Undine, anymore than there is for Lily. Whatever Undine acquires in the material world, Wharton tantalizes her with yet another delight just beyond her grasp.

Wharton questions the romantic ideal of escape in her depiction of male characters, as well. In *Ethan Frome*, the hero, a poor Berkshire Mountain farmer, is an extreme example of the price a male might have to pay for his desire to get beyond his community. After his mother's death, Ethan had turned for comfort to the first female in sight; thus he married a woman several years his senior, the woman who had nursed his mother in her final illness. Later when his wife Zeena is ill herself, she brings in a young female relative, Matty Silver, to nurse her; and the cycle begins to repeat itself. But to go away with Matty, he must abandon his social and marital obligations to his wife. When the two would-be lovers eventually find an escape, a way to get beyond, the route open to them is the one likewise open to Lily Bart, a form of suicide. That is to say, they have no identity outside their society, to escape is to annihilate themselves.

Later Wharton tells almost the same story about a wealthy Old New Yorker. Like Ethan Frome, Newland Archer in *The Age of Innocence* searches for a beyond to escape his wife and society. He has fallen in love with Ellen Olenska, an independent and sophisticated American woman who is already married, just as he has announced his engagement to her cousin May Welland, a naïve American "girl". After his marriage, he urges Olenska to flee with him to a place where adultery won't matter: "I want – I want somehow to get away with you into a world where words like that – categories like that – won't exist" (*AI*, 290). Olenska refuses to go with him beyond the constraints of Old New York because, unlike the inexperienced Matty Silver, she knows that such a world holds no promise for a woman. "Oh, my dear – where is that country?" she responds to his masculine naïveté, "Have you ever been there?" Her clear-headed thinking, which takes into account her relationship to Newland Archer but also their relationship to their communities in New York and Europe and to their marginalized existence in the world Newland proposes, is the mark, for Wharton, of maturity. Olenska insists on a compromise that denies their shared happiness, but allows her to live alone with dignity. It isn't a bad exchange, better certainly than the choice made by her literary sisters: Emma Bovary, Anna Karenina, even Edna Pontellier.

In later novels Wharton experiments with this theme by allowing her protagonists to escape and then charting their new course. In *The Mother's Recompense*, for example, the heroine Kate Clephane does abandon her family, a husband and three-year-old daughter, only to find that when she returns eighteen years later, she no longer has a place in New York or in her daughter's life; rather her identity is bound to Europe, the world of her exile. In another version of the theme, Halo Spears, the heroine of *The Gods Arrive*, is allowed to escape her husband and to flee to Europe with her lover Vance Weston. Once they arrive in European cities, however, they must accommodate themselves to the society there. The double-standard will allow Vance a place in various social circles, but Halo, as an adulteress, is excluded. She can only find her real identity by returning to America, even to her ancestral home, the Willows.

If society forms a bond around its individual members, it also provides a bond between the two, linking them in tacit agreement to fixed, shared values. Wharton's characters are shaped by social, biological and economic forces, but one could argue their final failures often result from choices. Lily Bart dies in poverty rather than spend the money she owes Gus Trenor or use Bertha Dorset's love letters to Lawrence Selden as blackmail to regain her social position. Ethan Frome, likewise, might have gone west with Matty Silver if he had been willing to abandon his wife to unbearable poverty and to lie to his friends in order to borrow money. Newland Archer might have eloped with Ellen Olenska before his marriage to May Welland, or he could have run away with her even after his wife announced her pregnancy, if Ellen Olenska had not agreed to the code of conduct implicit in Old New York society. Any society runs on the agreement of its members to abide by certain social and moral rules. Wharton's heroes and heroines usually adhere to that social covenant yet are, more often than not, defeated anyway. Adding to that irony is the fact that their society, while holding up the mask of respectability, never really takes the covenant seriously. Consequently, moral choices and sacrifices most often go unnoticed, undercutting their heroic potential.

Where is the community Wharton implicitly and, at times, explicitly promotes? In spite of the nostalgia of some of her later works, Wharton never found in American society her ideal community, a set of shared manners, morals, norms of behavior, patterns of conduct passed along from one generation to another that promote and enhance healthy social life. Lying under the harshness of Wharton's fictive world is what Judith Fryer calls an "urban pastoral"

(*Felicitous Space*, 115), a lament over the loss of an ideal community, a new Eden that would allow individuals, both male and female, to thrive within the social group. Yet the realist in Wharton cast a cold eye on the net or web, such as it was, and depicted the bitter compromises individuals must make to survive. Human nature, as she explained to Howells, came for her clad in social fabric.

3 *The House of Mirth* and the Question of Women

> We do not really know what women *are*.
> – Vernon Lee, Review of *Women and Economics*

> On his table lay the note: Lily had sent it to his rooms.
> He knew what was in it before he broke the seal – a
> grey seal with *Beyond!* beneath a flying ship. Ah, he
> would take her beyond – beyond the ugliness, the petti-
> ness, the attrition and corrosion of the soul –
> – Edith Wharton, *The House of Mirth*

In 1912 Wilbur Cross, the editor of the *Yale Review*, wrote
to Edith Wharton, asking her for an essay on the Woman
Question.[1] He had read her novels with care and was right
to believe that no one could probe beneath the surface
of the social issue more subtly and clearly than she.
Although he had chosen his essayist wisely, Wharton declined the offer, explaining that she did not feel prepared
to address the question of women. The analysis Cross
sought in discursive form had already been written, as he
must have known, in her fiction. The central issue in her
first novel about American society, *The House of Mirth*
(1905), is the Woman Question. Exploring the social and
economic conditions of turn-of-the-century women, like
those analyzed by Charlotte Perkins Gilman in *Women*

and Economics (1899), Wharton created a novel about the possibilities for female stories. As Vernon Lee put it in her review of Gilman's book: "We do not really know what women *are*." Wharton turns that declaration into a question, the one central to women of her day. If a woman chooses to discard the usual plot of marriage and her subsequent economic dependence on a man, then what? Exactly who is she? In more practical terms, how is she to earn her own way?

The heroine Lily Bart, a woman of rare sensibility, discernment and beauty, travels a course that should lead her to marriage, a union with male money and power, and yet she tarries along the way, escaping into the woods with the would-be romantic hero Lawrence Selden, whose chivalric impulse is to save her from the materialism of her society by guiding her to what he, having read and absorbed Emerson, calls "the republic of the spirit". We know that even before Lily encounters Selden's utopia, she has fancied an escape from the prosaic imperative to marry. She is twenty-nine as the novel opens, uncomfortably close to the barrier of thirty, when a man may begin to think about marriage, but beyond the time a woman may. We also know that Lily Bart seals her letters – epistolary contacts with the world around her – with the image of "Beyond! beneath a flying ship", a clear symbol of the romantic urge to "light out" for the territory or to take to the sea. Selden imagines a role for himself in her romantic quest: "Ah, he would take her beyond – beyond the ugliness, the pettiness, the attrition and corrosion of the soul – " (*HM*, 154). He seems indeed not to understand the ambivalent nature of the quest. If he succeeds in taking her "beyond" to the realm of personal freedom and autonomous selfhood, what are they to do once they arrive? To marry places them back in the social structure with the mundane questions of where and how to live on his income.

Over the course of the novel, two genres collide: the female domestic story and male pastoral romance. The traditional domestic story, as Nina Baym explains it in *Woman's Fiction*, tells a variation of one basic tale. A young woman, who in the opening of the novel is somehow deprived of support, finds that she must win her own way in the world. Through her energy, earnestness and self-reliance she is able to "perform dazzling exploits" and thereby gain for herself a happy ending, usually in a marriage which symbolizes "the successful accomplishment of the required task and resolutions of the basic problems raised in the story."[2]

The greatest happiness for both men and women comes from domestic relations, "the whole network of human attachments based on love, support, and mutual responsibility" (*Woman's Fiction*, 27). The hearth becomes the seat of power. Such a story is based on relational, not autonomous selfhood. It would seem from the opening scene that Wharton intends to tell such a story. Lily Bart, a fledgling member of the American leisure class, begins without the support of her parents and further loses the legacy she expects from her aunt. Left to win her own place, she flirts with the hero, a lawyer of relatively meager means. Both understand that a marriage between the two would not be in either's best interest, since they are too poor to support the union. They find throughout the course of the novel that though their match would be injudicious, they are nevertheless in love. The reader might expect that conflicting values, coincidental misunderstandings, and insufficient funds might be worked out over the course of the novel so that the marriage would, in the end, take place.

The pastoral romance posits an altogether different world, one beyond the quotidian world where individuals maneuver unfettered by the responsibilities attached to communal, heterosocial living. Lawrence Selden, the would-be romantic hero, feels it his duty to rescue the misguided Lily Bart from the domestic oppression of Old New York by playing Perseus to her Andromeda. Although Lily yearns for an ideal world free from social constraints, she must also be pragmatic. How is she to enter his "republic" and how might she live once there? A woman's life, she understands, differs significantly from a man's:

> If I were shabby no one would have me: a woman is asked out as much for her clothes as for herself. The clothes are the background, the frame, if you like: they don't make success, but they are a part of it. Who wants a dingy woman? (*HM*, 12)

Ironically, Selden himself doesn't want a "dingy woman"; he prefers fashionable Lily Bart to "dingy" Gerty Farish and, although he believes himself beyond New York society, he too has had an affair with its matriarch Bertha Dorset. Lily presses Selden with another practical question: Is the order celibate? "Not in the least," he responds, "though I'm bound to say there are not many married people in it" (*HM*, 69). Autonomous selfhood, freedom from "money, from poverty, from ease and anxiety, from all the material accidents" (*HM*, 68), stands at odds with relational selfhood, engagement with the social and, by necessity, the material world. Thus Selden, whose name uncomfortably collides with "seldom", is what Wharton herself called "a negative hero",[3] a man who, at crucial moments in the novel, squirms and retreats. Much as the hero and, at times, the heroine may want to feature in a pastoral romance, they find themselves rather in the clutches of a realistic social novel.[4]

As perhaps the best social historian of her day, Wharton studies the phenomenon of marriage in turn-of-the-century capitalist America, where the male barters to own a female and the female negotiates to secure a male. The novel presents the dilemma of the single woman, a capitalist commodity, who must earn her social place by enticing a wealthy male into marriage.

Lily Bart, whose name echoes the bartering going on throughout the novel, engages the reader's attention because she has through almost deliberate folly and inattention resisted such closure.[5] Social and biological necessity urges her, at twenty-nine, toward a quick solution to her problem. She might find shelter in the priggish arms of Percy Gryce, "who might ultimately decide to do her the honour of boring her for life" (*HM*, 25); or in the lecherous arms of Gus Trenor, who would play the stock market for her in exchange for sex. Or Lily could use her beauty to unseat her nemesis Bertha Dorset by wooing and winning her husband George. Finally, by using love letters that Bertha has written to Selden, Lily could blackmail the woman to secure her place in society and then marry the *arriviste* Simon Rosedale who would place her materially above her social counterparts for the privilege of owning her. Any of these men could provide her with the income she would need "to arrange her life as she pleased, to soar into that empyrean of security where creditors cannot penetrate" (*HM*, 77). All of these possible unions, which offer security at the price of financial dependency, are repugnant to her; the truth is that selling herself as a nuptial commodity has almost no appeal. The further question for her, for women in general, is: If not marriage, then what?

Edith Wharton feared that question. Feminists or "New Women" to her wore the visage of a "'monstrous regiment' of the emancipated; young women taught by their elders to despise the kitchen and the linen room, and to substitute the acquiring of University degrees for the more complex art of civilized living" (*BG*, 60). Perhaps the reason Wharton did not write the essay for Wilbur Cross is that she remained, in many ways, ambivalent. She did, for example, accept an honorary degree from Yale University in 1923, the first woman to be so honored. And she did see the disadvantages of the domestic and dependent female role. In *A Backward Glance*, for example, she lamented her lack of knowledge of her female forebears, gentlewomen who were "a toast" and little else.

In spite of her rhetoric, critics have long recognized Wharton's feminist leanings. Irving Howe, as early as 1962, sensed in her "a suppressed feminist bitterness, a profound impatience with the claims of the ruling sex."[6] Later Margaret McDowell in "Viewing the Custom of the Country: Edith Wharton's Feminism" (1974) noted Wharton's essential interest in the social plight of women in a male-dominated society.[7] Much has been done in the 1980s, first by Elizabeth Ammons in *Edith Wharton's Argument with America* (1980), to link Wharton to contemporary feminist thought. Ammons meticulously places Wharton's fiction in the context of the feminist texts of her day. Later Elaine Showalter in "The Death of the Lady (Novelist): Wharton's *House of Mirth*" (1985) and more recently Shari Benstock in *Women of the Left Bank* (1986) and Sandra Gilbert and Susan Gubar in *No Man's Land* (1989) have placed Wharton in the feminist canon, as a transitional figure between the nineteenth and twentieth centuries. None of these critics, however, has considered the more personal source of Wharton's feminism, her friendship with Vernon Lee, which may well have led her to the work of Charlotte Perkins Gilman.

"Intelligent women will never talk together when they can talk to men, or even listen to them", Edith Wharton explained in *French Ways and Their Meaning* (25). In spite of the seemingly anti-female, certainly anti-feminist thrust of that statement, Wharton made an exception with Vernon Lee, who was one of only three women who intimidated her with their knowledge in conversation. The Neapolitan journalist and novelist Matilde Serao and the

French poet Anna de Noilles were the other two (*BG*, 132). Wharton travelled to Il Palmerino (Maiano, Italy) in 1894 to meet Vernon Lee, a British scholar whose real name was Violet Paget. Lee overwhelmed the would-be novelist with her knowledge of Italian history (Lee had written *Studies of the Eighteenth Century in Italy*, *Belcaro*, and *Euphorian*), such background as Wharton would later use in her first novel, *The Valley of Decision* (1902).

After completing that novel, Wharton wrote to Howells in May 1902, asking him to intercede for her with *The North American Review* to accept her review of three plays about Francesca da Rimini (*Letters*, 61–2). Her review appeared in July 1902 alongside Vernon Lee's review of Charlotte Perkins Gilman's *Women and Economics*, a book for which Lee had also written the introduction (she refers to Gilman by her married name Stetson). We can reasonably assume Wharton read the review (she had even referred to Lee in her own article). While Wharton would have been reading the review, she was beginning to construct the tragic story of Lily Bart. "In what aspect could a society of irresponsible pleasure-seekers be said to have, on the 'old woe of the world', any deeper bearing than the people composing such a society could guess?" she asked herself (*BG*, 207). She found the answer in the Woman Question. "Its tragic implication lies in its power of debasing people and ideals. The answer, in short, was my heroine, Lily Bart," she declared. The pattern and rhetoric of the novel suggest the influence of Gilman and Lee's analysis of the problem on Wharton's fictional portrait.

"I believe that *Women and Economics* ought to open the eyes and, I think, also the hearts of other readers," Lee proclaimed in her review, "because it has opened my own to the real importance of what is known as the Woman Question." Lee favored Gilman's approach because it embraced both women and men, not women exclusively.

[T]he present condition of women – their state of dependence, tutelage, and semi-idleness; their sequestration
from the discipline of competition and social selection,
in fact their economic parasitism – is in itself a most
important factor in the wrongness of all our economic
arrangements.

The economic dependence of women on men stems from
sociological, not psychological, roots. Gilman theorized
that because women have had to spend their talents and
energies rearing children – infancy being increasingly
lengthened in humans as reason replaces instinct – women
have out of necessity attached themselves to men who can
provide support.

As a result, the woman has become the property of the
man. As Lee explained:

the woman thus dependent upon his activity and thus
appropriated to his children's service, becomes part and
parcel of the home, of the goods, of the children,
becomes appropriated to the nursing, the cooking, the
keeping in repair; becomes, thus amalgamated with the
man's property, a piece of property herself, body and
soul, a slave.

Both women and men suffer from the arrangement. For
women the parasitic bond results in "the wasting and per-
verting of virtues, the systematic misapplication of healthy
feelings and energies." Given the economic situation,
women are forced to use the power of sex – to become
"over-sexed" – in order to appeal to men, to prey on their
sexual appetites and thus gain their financial support. Lee
bemoaned "the time wasted, the bad covetousness excited,
the futile ingenuity exercised by the women who crowd
round the windows of our great shops" an image of what
Thorstein Veblen in *The Theory of the Leisure Class* (1899)

labelled the "conspicuous consumer". Men, consequently,
sacrifice the good of the community, and at times their
own good as well, to the material needs and cravings of
their wives and children. It is expensive to own such
chattel.

"I propose nothing", Lee declared, although in truth
she offered her own suggestions for change, adaptation
and evolution. She felt women needed more "functions",
including the opportunity to compete with men for employ-
ment. "We do not really know what women *are*", Lee
stressed. She ended with the image of an androgynous
female:

> if women attain legal and economic independence, if
> they get to live, bodily and intellectually and socially,
> a life more similar, I might say more symmetrical, to
> that of men, they will necessarily become – let us put
> it plainly, less attractive to possible husbands.

Social evolution would resolve that conflict, however, by
phasing out men who idealize the parasitic women, in favor
of those who accept the new model. In the end Vernon
Lee celebrated the Greek blend of aesthetic and athletic
vigor and loveliness, uniting Apollo and Athena in a single
androgynous figure, an idealization of Lesbos, an image
she herself adopted.

It is this analysis of marriage in America that forms the
core of Wharton's *House of Mirth*. Like her friend Vernon
Lee, she saw female dependency as a sociological problem
with ramifications for both women and men. The Bart
family, for example, suffers from the "economic parasitism" that Lee and Gilman described. Rather than
becoming a docile slave, Mrs Bart has become a crafty,
domineering exploiter of first her husband and then her
daughter. "The vigorous and determined figure" of the

mother ruled over the household "while the hazy outline
of a neutral-tinted father filled an intermediate space
between the butler and the man who came to wind the
clocks" (*HM*, 29). When Hudson Bart failed financially,
he became "extinct" to his wife, who turned to her
daughter's beauty as a new means of support. It is important to note, however, that Mrs Bart has no economic power
of her own; without her husband's money or that of some
other male who might, in a sense, purchase her daughter,
she has no way of providing a living for herself. She is
an economic parasite. Wharton's depiction of the distortions of the Bart family reveals her agreement with Gilman
and Lee that economic parasitism is unhealthy, even
perverse.

The mother has left her daughter with the "faith" that
"whatever it cost, one must have a good cook and be what
Mrs Bart called 'decently dressed'" (*HM*, 30). In the
marketplace terms of the novel, the "cost" amounts to
the withering of Lily's intelligence, strength and imagination, and the development of her beauty and sexuality,
more salable charms. As Lee put it, "The mischief lies
not in the fact of parasitism, but in the fact that this parasitic
life has developed in the parasite one set of faculties and
atrophied another." The parasitic woman fails to develop
faculties she may have had in common with men: intellect,
rationality, self-confidence. Lily thus gained from her
female training a hard exterior, a veneer of beauty and
highly polished manners, but remained "inwardly as
malleable as wax" (*HM*, 53), making it impossible for her
to rise above her economic dependency.

Wharton first titled the novel "A Moment's Ornament",
a suitable metaphor for her heroine, indeed for any leisure-
class woman of the era. If Wharton had used more of Lee's
rhetoric, she would have described Lily as "over-sexed".
Her real power, such as it is, is her sexuality. In spite
of advancing age and troubling rumors about her question-

able morality, Lily Bart stands at the height of her sexual power during the evening of *tableaux vivants* when she poses as Reynolds's "Mrs. Lloyd".[8] That parlor game, popular in late nineteenth century, allowed women to pose in varying states of semi-nudity under the name of "art" and allowed men to indulge in voyeurism. The portrait Lily selects features a tall, shapely female, draped in filmy cloth, which reveals as much as it conceals of her body. "Her pale draperies, and the background of foliage against which she stood, served only to relieve the long dryad-like curves that swept upward from her poised foot to her lifted arm" (*HM*, 134). As a true commodity, her thinly-veiled body gives her the only power she has in the novel over the men who surround her.

Yet as a commodity she has no real identity, rather she becomes the embodiment of each suitor's fantasy. To Selden her nearly nude body suggests a "touch of poetry", evoking in him "an overmastering longing to be with her again" (*HM*, 135). The nearly passionless hero is so moved by her sexuality, which he dares not even name, that he professes his love and pursues, for the only time in the novel, a passionate kiss. Ironically, Lily is left to ponder what she believes to be the sweetness of her power.

It attracts various other "suitors" as well. Gus Trenor claims the *tableau* is in "damned bad taste" (*HM*, 138), but does so only to mask his sexual attraction. He has tried unsuccessfully to purchase sexual favors from her by pretending to play the stock market for her. One of the dominant themes in the book is that everyone must "pay up". To get proper repayment from Lily, Gus tricks her into visiting his house alone at night to seduce or even rape her. Ironically the source of her power, her sexuality, places her in a powerless situation. Like Selden, Trenor finds her irresistible. He too longs to touch her, but "his touch was a shock to her drowning consciousness" and her scorn "called out the primitive man" (*HM*, 146). Only

Gus's sense of social taboo keeps him from raping Lily. Just as she has no financial power in the novel, she has no physical power to fight him off.

The third suitor Simon Rosedale arrives in the daylight at Aunt Peniston's house to make a legitimate offer. Just as attracted to Lily's sexuality as Selden and Trenor, Rosedale is less impulsive. He has taken more time to formulate his deal. "'I generally *have* got what I wanted in life, Miss Bart. I wanted money, and I've got more than I know how to invest; and now the money doesn't seem to be of any account unless I can spend it on the right woman'" (*HM*, 175). In order to get into New York society, he needs an appropriate woman to wear his finery and adorn his house, a female social savant who can manage his way into the exclusive recesses of New York society. In the terms we have been discussing the novel, Simon Rosedale is the most direct of the suitors. No poetry for him, nor rape, rather wise investment.

It takes even longer for the colorless, passive George Dorset to make his offer. His wife Bertha ironically lures Lily for him by asking her to come with them for a long vacation on their yacht. Lily understands that her job will be to keep George busy so that he will not notice that his wife is having another affair. George finally proposes to Lily by making another kind of deal: if she will help him unseat his faithless wife, he will divorce Bertha and marry Lily. What is most significant here to the question of female power is that the socially and economically strongest woman in the novel, Bertha Dorset, owes her power to her husband's money. Without him, she would lose her social place. That is why she must turn the tables on Lily by publicly ousting her from the yacht in order to maintain her marriage to a man she clearly doesn't love, doesn't even like or respect. In all its permutations, Wharton reveals the term "female power" as an oxymoron. Beauty and sexuality, those qualities the female must develop to attract the male, provide her in the end with no real power at all.

Lily Bart is a piece of property in New York society, the expensive piece of property Lawrence Selden notes in our first view of her. "He had a confused sense that she must have cost a great deal to make .... was it not possible that the material was fine, but that circumstance had fashioned it into a futile shape?" (*HM*, 7) That question echoes throughout the novel.[9] Rosedale's attraction to her springs from his appraisal of her as a commodity: "It was perhaps her very manner of holding herself aloof that appealed to his collector's passion for the rare and unattainable" (*HM*, 182–83). His "stock-taking" eyes make Lily "feel herself no more than some superfine human merchandise" (*HM*, 412). Gus Trenor, too, sees her in terms of a commodity that his money ought to be able to buy. In the would-be rape scene, he confronts her with what he sees as a simple business deal: "Hang it, the man who pays for the dinner is generally allowed to have a seat at table" (*HM*, 145).

The fact is that Lily Bart is nearly beyond the age of value as a social commodity. Her beauty and refinement are meant to be used to get a husband who will, in turn, support her. Without a male to depend on financially, Lily's options for making money become increasingly restricted. To resist a further economic fall, Lily must earn her own way if she does not want to be economically dependent on anyone. Her rebellion takes the form of a longing "to drop out of the race and make an independent life for herself." But, she asks herself, "what manner of life would it be?" (*HM*, 39)

In so doing, she asks the Woman Question. As Vernon Lee had pointed out, "We do not really know what women *are*." In working out the story of Lily's search for a "beyond", Wharton looks skeptically at the ideal of autonomous selfhood, the core of Selden's "republic of the spirit". Lily's quest for identity takes her "beyond" only during her pastoral chats with Selden in the woods. When she returns each time to society, she knows that the place "beyond" must still be in a community. The question for her once she, in a sense, renounces the leisure class, is where to go next, what other social group might she join. Here Wharton, like the female domestic novelists before her, defines her heroine in relational, not autonomous terms. As Wharton put the question to Howells: How much of life lies outside "the web of customs, manners, culture" spun about us? Selden and the male pastoral adventure cannot take Lily "beyond". Once outside Old New York society, she still has to earn her way by finding another community.

The community closest at hand is the "sisterhood" of philanthropic feminists, a group Lily might join through her friendship with the social worker Gerty Farish. As Lily puts it early in the novel, "What choice had she? To be herself, or a Gerty Farish" (*HM*, 25). While the wealth and privilege of the leisure class hold her imagination, Lily resists the life of the professional woman. Vernon Lee would have made Gerty the heroine, as Elaine Showalter has in her revisionist reading of the novel, because Gerty embodies economic independence, a model of the New Woman.[10]

In Wharton's novel, however, she is poor (at least, by Old New York standards), "mediocre", and "ineffectual" by Lily's estimate, and Wharton's as well. Gerty lacks the beauty and aesthetic sensibility of Lily Bart; "her eyes were of a workaday grey and her lips without haunting curves" (*HM*, 88). She lives in a "dingy", cramped flat and does philanthropic work; as an economically independent woman, she earns her own way. Wharton even turns Gilman and Lee's rhetoric around. If leisure-class women are economic "parasites", Gerty Farish is "a parasite in the moral order, living on the crumbs of other tables, and content to look through the window at the banquet spread for her friends" (*HM*, 149). In describing the New Woman, the economically independent woman, Wharton seems fearful of what her independence might cost. Wharton's echo of "parasitism" seems conscious: for a woman to become financially independent, she might indeed become, as Vernon Lee warned, less attractive to men. Although Gerty Farish loves Lawrence Selden, perhaps more than Lily does, she will never get the proposal Lily, with her beauty and sexuality, might expect.

> [Gerty] wanted happiness – wanted it as fiercely and unscrupulously as Lily did, but without Lily's power of obtaining it. And in her conscious impotence she lay shivering, and hated her friend – (*HM*, 163)

We know that Lily's power is illusory, but for all her independence Gerty still believes in the power of female beauty and sexuality.

It is Gerty who represents the "ethic of care" that Carol Gilligan sees as the center of female stories. When Lily, after her near rape, comes to Gerty for comfort, the motherly, nurturing, philanthropic urge wins over the jealous impulse. "Gerty's compassionate instincts, responding to the swift call of habit, swept aside all her reluctances" (*HM*, 163). They sleep for the night in the bonds of sisterhood with Gerty's arm under Lily, "pillowing her head in its hollow as a mother makes a nest for a tossing child" (*HM*, 167). That scene of female solidarity adumbrates Lily's deathbed scene at the end, when she holds the imaginary Struther baby. Such scenes suggest that Lily's quest is not for a world beyond, but rather for a world within the human community. They suggest, too, Wharton's own ambivalence about the Woman Question and power of feminists to affect social change.

If not Old New York and not a philanthropic sisterhood,

then where might the heroine find a place? The last fifty pages of the novel present other possibilities. Gerty and Carrie Fisher, united in their effort to secure a place for Lily, find a job for her in Mme Regina's millinery shop, alongside working-class women who have never known the luxury of being merely ornamental. The "fagged", "sallow", "dull and colourless" women work deftly in the "harsh" light and "unwholesome" air. Lily's goal is to join their ranks, to be "received as their equal", to join their community. But she finds herself physically and psychologically unfit for work, as a result of what Gilman and Lee warned against, the atrophying of certain skills. Lily has never been trained to do even the most perfunctory of female chores, her "untutored fingers" cannot sew the stitches necessary to trim hats. Wharton's narrator explains Lily's failure in sociological terms:

> It was bitter to acknowledge her inferiority even to herself, but the fact had been brought home to her that as a bread-winner she could never compete with professional ability. Since she had been brought up to be ornamental [an echo of the first title], she could hardly blame herself for failing to serve any practical purpose. (*HM*, 480)

The workroom is not her environment. The same conditions under which her co-workers operate cause Lily to become ill.

Lily seeks other communities in her last two days. She journeys back to Selden's apartment, willing to burn Bertha's letters, her last chance to regain her place in the leisure class, and willing as well to accept the economically lesser place as Selden's wife. She visits the Struthers and finds comfort in their simple, but clean kitchen. In the scene with the Struthers, the novel gives us the kind of marriage found in female domestic novels, but not the heroine's marriage, as readers might expect. George Struther, a simple working man, has accepted Nettie Crane Struther's affair with another man; we are invited to measure his willingness to accept Nettie against our hero Lawrence Selden's inability to accept the affair he mistakenly thinks he sees going on between Lily and Gus Trenor. Both Nettie and George work; the baby is in the care of a sitter. Clear from Wharton's portrait of a successful marriage is the fact that neither partner is economically dependent on the other, rather together they have built a nest "on the edge of a cliff". The "central truth of existence", as Lily comes to see it, is community: "a mere wisp of leaves and straw, yet so put together that the lives entrusted to it may hang safely over the abyss" (*HM*, 320). This domestic scene comes as a surprise in the novel; we have only a glimpse of Nettie Crane earlier in the novel and no forewarning that her situation will be at all significant. The clean kitchen, devoted husband and healthy baby all seem more the product of a domestic story, somewhat sentimentally rendered. Yet they do present for Lily a *tableau* of one possibility for living within a community.

When she returns to her boarding house, Lily has been so moved by the Struthers' sense of community that she is even willing for the first time to go down to dinner with the other boarders, another attempt to find a new social place for herself. Finally before the drug dulls her senses she discovers in her suffering a bond with all others who have likewise suffered before her: "If only life could end now – end on this tragic yet sweet vision of lost possibilities, which gave her a sense of kinship with all the loving and foregoing in the world!" (*HM*, 321) It is clearly "kinship" Lily seeks.

Once beyond her social group, she cannot secure a place in a new one. That loss of human contact makes her literally ill. To place herself outside the circle is to swing "unsphered in a void of social non-existence".

Lily, for all her dissatisfied dreaming, had never really conceived the possibility of revolving about a different centre: it was easy enough to despise the world, but decidedly difficult to find any other habitable region. (*HM*, 262)

Not to find a "habitable region" is to be "expatriate everywhere". In describing her plight, Lily employs the rhetoric of the determinist writers of Wharton's day:

> I can hardly be said to have an independent existence. I was just a screw or a cog in the great machine I called life, and when I dropped out of it I found I was of no use anywhere else. What can one do when one finds that one only fits into one hole? (*HM*, 498)

Lily comes to rely more and more on the drug chloral to dull the effects of the pain of her separation. The narrator explains that "in the sleep which the phial procured" Lily "sank into depths of dreamless annihilation" (*HM*, 294–5). To get "beyond" to a realm outside the human community, the novel suggests, is to "annihilate" the self.

Lily's seal "Beyond! beneath a flying ship" symbolizes an impossible quest, the romantic flight to another world. The flying ship metaphor and sea imagery run throughout the novel. Old New York society is described as a flowing current. Outside Mrs Peniston's window, for example, figures with money and therefore power rise "to the surface with each recurring tide" (*HM*, 120). Without money or the prospects of a wealthy husband, Lily feels herself in "dark seas"; whenever pressures subside she feels "enough buoyancy to rise once more above her doubts" (*HM*, 87). When Selden receives her note, sealed with "*Beyond!* beneath a flying ship", he imagines himself Perseus rescuing Andromeda who "clings to him with dragging arms as he beats back to land with his burden" (*HM*,

158–9). He realizes he must take them through "not, alas, a clean rush of waves", but instead "a clogging morass of old associations and habits".

As Lily's hopes to rise above her situation fail, the sea metaphors become more frightening, adumbrating her end as a castaway and eventually a suicide. After her ouster from Old New York society, during a brief encounter with Judy Trenor in a restaurant, Lily takes the measure of her fate: "Where Judy Trenor led, all the world would follow; and Lily had the doomed sense of the castaway who has signalled in vain to fleeing sails" (*HM*, 229). When facing her Aunt Peniston's rejection of her, an act that will leave her practically penniless, Lily senses that confiding in Selden would be "as seductive as the river's flow to the suicide" (*HM*, 173). "The first plunge would be terrible – " she thinks, "but afterward, what blessedness might come!"

As Selden returns to Lily at the end of the novel, coming to her apartment as she had come to his at the beginning, the sea imagery returns. If Lily is painted as a castaway, then Selden is her sea-faring rescuer. As he hastened down her squalid street, he senses a youthful adventure: "He had cut loose from the familiar shores of habit, and launched himself on uncharted seas of emotion; all the old tests and measures were left behind, and his course was to be shaped by new stars" (*HM*, 324). In the most bitterly ironic scene in the novel, the hero has finally found the word he meant to say, just as she had died the night before with the word on her lips.

The word that passes between the living hero and the dead heroine in the final scene is never given. Critics often read the word as "love" or "faith". These choices allow for a literal interpretation of the scene; the hero has come, albeit belatedly, to profess his "love" and the heroine responds, albeit from the grave, that "love" has been her word as well. Robin Beaty, in "Lilies that Fester" (1987),

places the last scene within the tradition of women's sentimental fiction and argues that Wharton's use of such stock
sentimentality lessens the realism of the novel.[11] Over the
course of the novel, however, Wharton has revised the
usual plots of both the female domestic or sentimental
novel and the male pastoral romance.

We might also read the word as it is not written, the
message as a non-message. The hero and heroine are
"beyond" communication. The suggestion of the word
"beyond" ties together the several elements of the novel
that I have been discussing. Its absence leaves the novel
without resolution. Even if we place "beyond" in the void
as the word that passes between the dead heroine and
live hero, it continues to leave the parting message in question. It is Lily's motto throughout the novel, the symbol
of her quest to escape from society and create a self outside
the group. The use of the word at the end echoes its initial
placement "beneath a flying ship" on Lily's seal and thereby unites the sea imagery that runs throughout the novel.
In a sense, both Lily and Selden have found ways to "cut
loose from the familiar shores of habit." They have
launched themselves on new "uncharted seas". Ironically,
their voyages differ greatly.

If we read "beyond" from Lily's point of view, we see
that she has fallen prey to poverty, illness, depression and
drugs. Her final vision of "beyond", seemingly the only
escape left, is the longing for death. If we read the word
from Selden's point of view, we see that he remains moored
in his "republic of the spirit", a romantic escape from the
society surrounding him. He imagines Lily's seal and the
word "Beyond!" as their parting message, an other-
worldly linking of spirits. His reading allows for a literal
and sentimental interpretation. The reader, "beyond" the
confines of the novel, still must grapple with the reality
of Lily's death and the impossibility, given the realism of
the novel, that the two lovers can any longer communicate.

Even if they could send the "word", Wharton's irony reminds us, they would still fail to understand each other.

Lily Bart is the heroine of *The House of Mirth*, and not Gerty Farish or Nettie Crane Struther, or even Bertha Dorset or Judy Trenor, because Wharton finally had no answer to the Woman Question; as she explained to Wilbur Cross as late as 1912, she was not prepared to deal with its possible answers. She understood, as Charlotte Perkins Gilman and Vernon Lee did, that the woman's economic dependence on her society, specifically on men, left her vulnerable to the power of a frivolous, if not evil, society. In constructing that story about American society, Wharton resisted the usual domestic plot of happiness through marriage, yet she remained equally skeptical of the solutions offered by romance. She saw "Beyond! beneath a flying ship" as a futile quest.

4 *The Custom of the Country* and the Atlantic's Call

But Miss Wincher's depreciatory talk had opened ampler vistas, and the pioneer blood in Undine would not let her rest. She had heard the call of the Atlantic seaboard, and the next summer found the Spraggs at Skog Harbour, Maine.

        – Edith Wharton, *The Custom of the Country*

To the young woman confronting life there is the same world beyond [as there is to the young man], there are the same human energies and human desires and ambitions within. But all that she may wish to have, all that she may wish to do, must come through a single channel and a single choice. Wealth, power, social distinction, fame – not only these, but home and happiness, reputation, ease and pleasure, her bread and butter – all, must come to her through a small gold ring.

        – Charlotte Perkins Gilman, *Women and Economics*

The American story, as it has featured in male adventure stories and pastoral romances, posits westward expansion as the literal and figurative ideal, the manifest destiny of a nation severed from the constricting social structures of Europe. The "territory" lay waiting for colonization, luring the pioneer with limitless possibilities for freedom, money, power. When Edith Wharton and other women told the American story, their version often differed fundamentally from that of their male colleagues. Wharton's characters seek community, not autonomy; their quest, more often than not, is to find a place in the social world, to "fit" as snugly as possible and thus secure their survival, even their success. The heroine of *The Custom of the Country* Undine Spragg, as a female "pioneer", listens for and responds to "the call of the Atlantic" and the civilized as passionately as male pioneers had heard the call of the Pacific and "the wild".

No Wharton character more epitomizes the female quest for social power and position than Undine. She comes from Wharton's version of the socially nebulous Midwest, where cities are called Deposit, Opake and Apex (Wharton herself never visited the Midwest or West and her satiric portraits of those regions reveal her east-coast bias).[1] Undine learns early that such society is dull, unimaginative and removed from the socially stratified and culturally complex cities of the East. By manipulating her doting parents, the child Undine begins her quest for upward social mobility: "Her first struggle – after she had ceased to scream for candy, or sulk for a new toy – had been to get away from Apex in summer" (*CC*, 52). The Spraggs do move beyond Apex to summer resorts, first on a midwestern lake, later to Virginia and Maine, eventually to New York and Paris. Yet Undine finds that there is always another "beyond"; each new society offers further promise of vistas Undine has not yet imagined. Just as she believes herself to have reached the summit, Undine's happiness is spoiled by "a peep through another door" or "a new glimpse into the unimagined" (*CC*, 54–5). Her destiny is eastward, not westward bound; she travels back through the mystifying layers of culture, searching all along for clues to the "hieroglyphic" worlds of the New York leisure class and the European aristocracy:

All was blurred and puzzling to the girl in this world of half-lights, half-tones, eliminations and abbreviations; and she felt a violent longing to brush away the cobwebs and assert herself as the dominant figure of the scene. (*CC*, 37)

Over the course of the novel, Undine battles her way upward through the social labyrinth by learning the codes that allow her to master an economic and social system designed to enslave her.

Undine Spragg is a *femme fatale* whose untiring energy proves to be a force fatal to men, even literally so to her second husband, Ralph Marvell.[2] All of her energy, the novel illustrates, finally goes into her "business", the buying and trading of husbands. As Gilman pointed out, although as a woman Undine may seek a "beyond" with all the energy and earnestness a man may bring to such a quest, her final and only vehicle is marriage:

Wealth, power, social distinction, fame – not only these, but home and happiness, reputation, ease and pleasure, her bread and butter – all, must come to her through a small gold ring.[3]

However, rather than a passive victim of "economic parasitism", she, like her literary foremothers Mrs Bart and Bertha Dorset, is a crafty and determined exploiter, a tireless female pioneer.

Her pioneering forefathers were rootless, drifting men who moved from job to job seizing any opportunity to make money. Undine's grandfather had made and lost money as an undertaker, then a minister, and finally a druggist and inventor of a hair-waver. Her father took over what was left of the family fortune after his father-in-law had lost nearly everything speculating in land. Abner Spragg was able to rebuild the fortune in the ironically named "Pure Water" movement, the financial deal that continues throughout the novel, mysteriously bringing billions of dollars to many men in a series of impure business maneuvers. Once they have money, the Spraggs journey to the East, following the lure of the Atlantic, and in the female offspring Undine the family retraces their historical path back to Europe. In the process of pioneering the New Land, they have lost contact with the European culture that had produced them. Like so many immigrants to America, the goal had been to blend by rounding the edges and the Spraggs, by discovering how to fit, had managed to win a clear place in Apex. The harder task for them all is to return to the culture their pioneering forebears had abandoned.

As Mr Spragg might have launched a son (had his son lived) into the family business, teaching him how to pressure politicians, bully colleagues and negotiate deals, so he launches his daughter on her career, the female version of his own. Undine is the suitable heir; the Spragg money goes to back her career. As an American "businesswoman" Undine pressures, bullies and negotiates her way into élite society by marrying, divorcing and remarrying wealthy, powerful men. While her father attends to the earning and securing of family wealth, Undine earns and secures family social position. Her vocation is to translate the money of Wall Street into the luxury of Fifth Avenue.

In creating Undine, Wharton responded to the social theory of her day. Her heroine is the "conspicuous consumer" that Thorstein Veblen described in his *Theory of the Leisure Class* (1899). The turn-of-the-century leisure-class wife, Veblen contended, moves "under the guidance of traditions that have been shaped by the law of conspicuously wasteful expenditure of time and substance."[4] The status of a family is marked by their consumption of material goods and the job of the woman in such a system is to become "the ceremonial consumer". His analysis, published the same year as *Women and Economics*, made essentially the same appraisal of American marriage that Gilman's study did. Wharton's heroine Undine Spragg can see only the surface of the world and thus never feels that she is demeaned by her social role, rather she glories in it. Wharton offers a bitingly satirical "portrait of a lady" whose success serves to reveal to the reader a portrait of a corrupt social and economic system. As Ammons points out in *Edith Wharton's Argument with America*, the real object of attack in the novel is not the heroine "self-centered and insensitive as she is, but the institution of marriage in the leisure class" (101–2). Given the "customs, manners, culture" of turn-of-the-century America, Wharton is saying, Undine is ironically the heroine.

Wharton elaborates on the imbalance in the human community caused by *laissez-faire* capitalism and the resulting division between male and female spheres. In another irony, a male character, Charles Bowen, explains a version of the social theory to a woman, Ralph Marvell's sister Laura Fairford, in their discussion of "the whole problem of American marriages" (*CC*, 205–8). A male tells the story to a female, I suppose, because a man is privy to male attitudes and manners. Women, in this system, are depicted as naïve, infantilized by their inferior social position separate from the sphere of adult, male responsibility.

The essential weakness in the nuptial bond, so Bowen theorizes, is "that the average American looks down on his wife." Note that for him "the average American" is a man. In marriage, the man is expected to provide all monetary, material goods for his wife and later for their children. Such a task takes him away from the home, out into the world of "business", a corrupt, competitive, grinding world of deals, persuasions, coercions and double-deals with the making of money at the center. Love for a woman or desire for a balanced marital union, even interest in a friendship with a woman or attraction to a heterosocial community all have no value to the businessman, who devotes himself instead to an affair with money. "In America the real *crime passionnel* is a 'big steal' – there's more excitement in wrecking railways than homes" (*CC*, 207), Bowen explains.

In the male passion for business and his companionship in the homosocial world of male competition and intrigue, the woman is left out of the picture. "The custom of the country," Bowen enlightens us about the novel's title, is that men tell their women nothing of the workings of their business life. The women, as a result, never understand the nature or extent of their responsibility in the marriage. Rather the male selects a female to wear his wealth; the woman becomes, in a sense, little more than another acquisition. The male does not give her the information that will allow her to become an equal partner, nor does he take any interest in her life, the world the female has created with the wealth at her disposal. The heart of Bowen's argument, and I think it fair to say Wharton's as well, is that the human community fails between men and women because nowhere is there open, honest, clear communication. "And what's the result – how do the women avenge themselves?" Bowen asks rhetorically, in one of the most pointedly didactic sections of the novel:

All my sympathy's with them, poor deluded dears, when I see their fallacious little attempts to trick out the leavings tossed them by the preoccupied male – the money and the motors and the clothes – and pretend to themselves and each other that *that's* what really constitutes life! (*CC*, 208)

The material luxuries "given" to women in exchange for the silent acceptance of their secondary social position amount to a "big bribe".

The imbalance between men and women grows out of

social conditions; Wharton's message here is exactly the one she uses as the basis of Lily Bart's tragic fall in *The House of Mirth*. The woman fails to mature in that her powers of intellect, rationality, imagination all atrophy so that other traits may grow strong; to survive socially she must use her beauty and sexuality to attract a wealthy man, who will provide her a place in society. The difference between *The House of Mirth* and *The Custom of the Country* is in the depiction of the heroines. Although much of the first novel is satirically drawn – Percy Gryce, for example, or Aunt Peniston and Grace Stepney – it is at heart a tragedy, highlighting Lily's social and physical decline. The second novel is, in spite of the tragic death of the hero Ralph Marvell, a satire; Undine's social "climb" is undercut continually by the exposure of her quest as sham.

How we come to see the heroines points up the difference between them. Lily has a hard exterior but is "inwardly as malleable as wax" while Undine is "malleable outwardly" but inwardly "insensible to the touch of the heart" (*CC*, 224). Lily begins with an original style and clear aesthetic sense; she knows instinctively how to dress, when to speak, the tone to use. Undine, who begins her career at the appropriately named Stentorian Hotel has no knowledge at all of the subtleties of leisure-class manners, costume, or custom; she must learn what Lily already knows. Both heroines possess remarkable beauty and graceful lines; the important difference is how we, as readers, come to see them. We view Lily's beauty through the eyes of others, first Lawrence Selden, and later other male suitors and women too, especially Gerty Farish. Even during her *tableau vivant* when she pantomimes Reynold's "Mrs Lloyd", Lily's true self shines through her disguise.

We see Undine Spragg, however, through her own eyes. Whenever she walks through a room, she stops to look at her own reflection in a mirror. Undine continually positions and repositions herself to alter the contours of her surface, the "light" and "mirror" show of a confidence (wo)man. Her crafty changeability has grown from her favorite childhood game of "dressing up" and parading before the mirror, a "secret pantomime" (*CC*, 22). She glides and sways, twists and sparkles before the mirror to draw "fresh hope from the sight of her beauty" (*CC*, 245). Ralph attributes her "Narcissus-element" to her youth and assumes that she will outgrow the need for such approval as she matures. He is right that her passion for the mirror comes from her need to see "her own charm mirrored" in the admiration of others (*CC*, 157). Although she ages through the course of the novel, Undine never matures; Wharton illustrates her continued immaturity through her inability to see past the mirror or past the "image of herself in other minds which was her only notion of self-seeing" (*CC*, 401).

Unlike Lily Bart who fails finally to fit into a community, Undine Spragg not only survives but succeeds by fitting into several social groups. Her skill in fitting herself into society comes from her ability to alter her surface image. For example, when she unexpectedly meets the family of the Frenchman, Raymond de Chelles, who will become her third husband, Undine shows herself to be a quick study:

> She was used to such feats of mental agility, and it was instinctive with her to become, for the moment, the person she thought her interlocutors expected her to be: but she had never had quite so new a part to play at such short notice. (*CC*, 386)

Her lessons before the mirror had prepared her to change disguises with ease and agility, a craft necessary to her "business".

Undine sets out to learn the knowledge that Lily already understands – the subtleties of gesture and nuance, the grace of genteel social custom, the myriad messages beneath the surface of conversation. After years of hard work, Undine sees herself as superior to her set of *nouveaux riches*:

> It was not merely her title and her "situation", but the experiences she had gained through them, that gave her this advantage over the loud vague company. She had learned things they did not guess: shades of conduct, turns of speech, tricks of attitude – and easy and free and enviable as she thought them, she would not for the world have been back among them at the cost of knowing no more than they. (*CC*, 558)

Wharton's satiric humor comes from such irony; it is Undine who believes herself "superior" yet her "success" begs the question: Who would care to reign over such a throng?

Inwardly, as well as outwardly, Lily and Undine differ. Lily fails to rise socially and economically because she is unwilling to accept the ethics of Wall Street; if she had blackmailed Bertha Dorset with her love-letters to Lawrence Selden, she too could have asserted herself as "the dominant figure in the scene". Her refusal to adopt the morally shady ethics of her culture, the tactics of the business world, causes her expulsion from the community. Undine, however, accepts the maxim that "every Wall Street term [has] its equivalent in the language of Fifth Avenue." She succeeds where Lily has failed because she willingly adopts the amorality, and even immorality, of business.

Lily Bart is unschooled in business, unable to plan, manage and negotiate deals in her best interest; Undine Spragg can do all these things shrewdly. Beneath the heavy brows she inherited from her father, Undine studies, guides, manipulates and controls the social world around her. She is the successful business woman, if we consider, as Wharton invites us to, marriage as the female "business". A woman's career in the economic and social configuration of American culture, Wharton's novel illustrates, is to find a male to protect her from financial disaster, a man who can provide all the material comforts that place her above the laborious, mundane task of earning her own money. What if, the novel asks us to consider, a woman has the savvy to figure out her place and the will to gain as much power in it as possible?

All of Undine's female "colleagues" from her mid-western town of Apex come to understand, as Gilman argued, that marriage is their vehicle; their social position is marked by a "gold ring" that represents their husband's financial success. To move socially and financially upward, a woman must move beyond the situation of her first marriage; that initial "deal" may well land her a better position, but the next question is how to get a "promotion". Either her husband must successfully struggle upward or the wife must find a wealthier mate, a new man who already has superior rank. To free herself from the old bond, if her husband doesn't die as Ralph did, the woman must divorce the man who holds her back.

Indiana Frusk, "the freckled daughter of the plumber 'across the road'" (CC, 22), learns that she can control her fate only by divorcing and remarrying. Beginning her "career" with Undine's castoff Millard Binch, she later sheds him for James Rolliver, a financial power. In one of the novel's most humorous passages, Indiana Frusk Binch Rolliver urges discretion on Undine, who has had an imprudent affair with Peter Van Degen before cinching their marital deal.

"I could have told you one thing right off," Mrs Rolliver

went on with her ringing energy. "And that is, to get your divorce first thing. A divorce is always a good thing to have: you never can tell when you may want it. You ought to have attended to that before you even *began* with Peter Van Degen." (*CC*, 346)

Undine learns two lessons from her miscalculation with Van Degen: first, never give into a man's passion before he is caught; and second, never divorce one man without a clear and better catch secured. This scene is characteristic of Wharton's satiric humor. She continues to play on the initial irony by moving from the satiric to the absurd. Indiana's new marriage, the narrator explains, is as real as the pearls thrown in by Rolliver to purchase his wife "if she kept out of certain states". Presumably, there are some states left, Wharton implies, that would not recognize this "business" as legitimate. Moving to the absurd, Wharton concludes with Indiana's denunciation of the New York reticence to divorce on, of all things, moral grounds: "Thank goodness I was brought up in a place where there's some sense of decency left!" (*CC*, 347).

Wharton's novels argue strongly that human beings seek identity within a group and draw a sense of self from their relationship one with another. The bitter tone of *The Custom of the Country* comes from Wharton's conviction that human community has failed in America. Undine Spragg stands metaphorically for the United States itself, as her initials suggest. Typical of her compatriots, Undine is "fiercely independent and yet passionately imitative": she "wanted to surprise every one by her dash and originality, but she could not help modelling herself on the last person she met" (*CC*, 19).

Her conflict produces the confusion of ideals that Wharton believed to be at the root of American tradition, without a sense of its own history. Moreover, perpetual discontent undercuts Undine's sizeable materialistic achievements. That is Wharton's ultimate criticism of the American quest for change, progress, social evolution, individual mobility; such movement leaves no resting place, no haven for the individual wanderer, no final sense of achievement or satisfaction. Over nearly 600 pages, Undine blazes and glitters, yet remains discontented: "She had learned that there was something she could never get, something that neither beauty nor influence nor millions could ever buy for her" (*CC*, 594). Wharton dangles before her heroine the social position of an ambassadress, a position that, in Undine's day, her divorces prevent her from attaining: "she said to herself that it was the one part she was really made for." She's right, of course; the ultimate irony of the novel is that Undine is an ambassadress, the representative American woman.

The confusion of ideals is heightened by the oxymoronic quality of the name itself. The name Undine, like undulation, suggests movement while the surname Spragg denotes stasis, a piece of wood used to block the wheel of a vehicle to prevent its backward movement on an incline. Undine cannot fall or fail because she begins with her father's financial backing. At the same time, she can never be content to stop. Her ceaseless motion upward, buttressed by Spragg's money and social position, combine to symbolize Wharton's assessment of the American character.

The name, too, alludes to an undine, a female water sprite, who according to folklore, can acquire a soul and thus become human, by marrying and having a child by a mortal.[5] Furthering the irony is the fact that Undine's wealth is born from the "Pure Water" movement in Apex. In the novel Undine's fluctuating nature, her undulations, attract the attention of numerous men, all mortals who could humanize her, as the myth goes. "*Diverse et ondoyante*" she appears to the romantic Ralph Marvell. He sees in her name the French phrase and moves toward his vision of her. Her mother, however, explains the more prosaic root of her name; Undine was the name Mrs Spragg's father had given to his invention, a "hair-waver", "from *un*doolay . . . the French for crimping" (*CC*, 80). The utilitarian hair curler is, in the end, a closer metaphor, a mechanical device to force unnatural beauty.

The novel focuses on Undine's second marriage as the primary example of how human community fails in American society. The love story begins with a series of confrontations, meetings between middle-class mid-westerners and leisure-class easterners. Neither group escapes ridicule. Undine is introduced as a spoiled, willful, determined young woman, whose chief interest is herself, not the remote inner regions of her intellect or imagination, but rather the surface of her face and body. As she parades before the mirror, Wharton humorously details her concern:

Only one fact disturbed her: there was a hint of too much fulness in the curves of the neck and in the spring of her hips. She was tall enough to carry off a little extra weight, but excessive slimness was the fashion, and she shuddered at the thought that she might some day deviate from the perpendicular. (*CC*, 23)

Her concern with the surfaces of life causes her to puzzle over trivia, for example, what kind of stationery to use in her response to Marvell's sister's invitation to dine. In "Boudoir Chat" she has learned that "the smartest women were using the new pigeon-blood notepaper with white ink," but Laura Fairford, a wealthy and supposedly fashionable woman, for some mysterious reason has used an "old-fashioned white sheet" (*CC*, 18). The puzzle over manners is later heightened when, in the meeting between Undine and Laura, they discuss the arts.

Undine did not even know that there were any [art exhibits] to be seen, much less that "people" went to see them; and she had read no new book but "When the Kissing Had to Stop", of which Mrs Fairford seemed not to have heard. On the theatre they were equally at odds, for while Undine had seen "Oolaloo" fourteen times, and was "wild" about Ned Norris in "The Soda-Water Fountain", she had not heard of the famous Berlin comedians who were performing Shakespeare at the German Theatre . . . (*CC*, 37)

These humorous clashes between manners, aesthetics and cultural values suggest to the reader a point missed by the hero Ralph Marvell. How can a marriage between two such fundamentally different social beings possibly last for long?

The clash in manners, tastes and customs between social groups has always been the source of action in novels of manners. As Lionel Trilling put it in his influential essay, "Manners, Morals, and the Novel", the novel of manners takes as its subject social manners, "a culture's hum and buzz of implication". Manners are "that part of a culture which is made up of half-uttered or unuttered or unutterable expressions of value."[6] He contends that American society has failed to produce novels of manners because of the thinness of the culture and the ideological resistance to explaining life in the social context. In *Custom of the Country*, as well as her other social novels, Wharton is demonstrating that American society indeed has enough social stratification, or "hum and buzz", to allow her this *métier*.[7] The clash not only reveals the difference between Undine's sense of culture and that of the Marvell/Fairfords, it also measures the distance between what the would-be romantic hero Ralph Marvell thinks he is getting in Undine Spragg and the reality of his choice.

Ralph is not exempt from the novel's satire. As a child

he had explored his inner, not his outer, world. Undine posed before the mirror, but Ralph, a romantic hero, retreated to a secret cave at the seaside: "a secret inaccessible place with glaucous lights, mysterious murmurs, and a single shaft of communication with the sky" (*CC*, 76). While Undine was hanging on the fence in Apex with Indiana Frusk, Ralph was attending Harvard and Oxford, travelling through Europe and reading law. As Cynthia Griffin Wolff has argued, Wharton's portrait of a gentleman contains her most "devastating comment on the world of her childhood" (*A Feast of Words*, 239). His education was not meant to prepare him to do anything but dabble in the arts and perhaps write a few poems.

> The only essential was that he should live "like a gentleman" – that is, with a tranquil disdain for mere money-getting, a passive openness to the finer sensations, one or two fixed principles as to the quality of wine, and an archaic probity that had not yet learned to distinguish between private and "business" honour. (*CC*, 75)

Wharton's satiric definition of the "gentleman", which reduces supposedly superior social refinement to the ability to waste time and select wine, suggests that Ralph must share the responsibility for his own failure.

In this novel, as in *The House of Mirth*, the male romantic quest is revealed as immature folly. In a clear echo of Lawrence Selden's maritime fantasies, Ralph Marvell hoped someday to "launch his own boat" (*CC*, 77). His courtship of Undine likewise resembles Selden's fantasy about Lily Bart. In "a whirl of metaphor" (*HM*, 159), Selden uses the language and images of mythology to express his romantic quest to take Lily beyond the material world, a Perseus rescuing Andromeda. Ralph uses the exact scene to imagine his heroic rescue of Undine:

[H]e seemed to see her like a lovely rock-bound Andromeda, with the devouring monster Society careering up to make a mouthful of her; and himself whirling down on his winged horse – just Pegasus turned Rosinante for the nonce – to cut her bonds, snatch her up, and whirl her back into the blue... (*CC*, 84)

Ralph, like Selden, desires a romantic escape from the prosaic restrictions of life. The force of the humor in the first section of *The Custom of the Country* comes from the unwitting mismatch of such utterly different people. In this novel, Wharton gives her romantic hero what he thinks he wants. Ralph takes his "Andromeda" away from society on a long honeymoon in the remote, scenic regions of Italy only to find that crowded, noisy hotels are her element. Undine lives before the mirror as he does in his cave. Such a union, Wharton's satire insists, can never work.

The Custom of the Country inverts the plot of *The House of Mirth* in significant ways. Although Lily, by avoiding marriage, comes before her death to understand "the central truth" of human community, Undine, by using every marital opportunity to her material advantage, never comes to understand community at all. The heroes too have opposite fates. Unlike Selden, who is allowed to live with his illusions, Ralph comes to a painful and fatal realization. As Elmer Moffatt, Undine's first and fourth husband, puts it to him when he explains that Undine has also been his wife: "It's mighty wholesome for a man to have a round now and then with a few facts" (*CC*, 466).

His comment reflects Wharton's own philosophizing in *French Ways and Their Meaning*: "The 'sheltered life,' whether of the individual or of the nation, must either have a violent and tragic awakening – or never wake up at all" (66). The price of Ralph's facing "a few facts" is his suicide; he cannot live as a mature male in a world he must see clearly. Men, as well as women, may be victims of a "frivolous society", Wharton's novel argues. "Economic parasitism" may prove fatal to the male as well as the female; a woman need not acquiesce, indeed she may overpower her master.

Marriage, the primary heterosocial as well as sexual union, is depicted as a business. But that is not necessarily a negative comparison in Wharton's fiction. The Struther marriage, for example, in *The House of Mirth* is one of the few successes because Nettie and George are, in a sense, business partners, each shares in the outside labor and in the care of the child; through partnership they build their "nest" over the "abyss". Undine complains to Elmer Moffatt that the French also view marriage as a business: "They think so differently about marriage over here: it's just a business contract" (*CC*, 570). Her third husband Raymond de Chelles does expect Undine to be a partner, understanding and accepting the responsibilities of marriage, thinking of the good of the group before her own desire. Undine's notion of marriage, her "business", is an altogether different one, based on financial and social competition. The female baits and catches the male who then must "slave" for her, while she ignores the practicalities of money and work.

Undine's third and fourth marriages serve to complete Wharton's study of the modern marriage. Raymond de Chelles, like Ralph, is attracted to Undine's surface, her light and energy. She works hard to change her outward form in order to please him, his sister and his mother. Once married to Raymond, however, Undine learns that her beauty and sexuality can do nothing to alter the traditional life of the French community. The force of history is stronger than her temporal charms:

Dynasties had fallen, institutions changed, manners and morals, alas, deplorably declined; but as far back as

memory went, the ladies of the line of Chelles had always
sat at their needle-work on the terrace of Saint Desert
... (*CC*, 514)

Her resistance to the family claim for mutual assistance,
her refusal to understand family finances, her failure to
follow Raymond's intellectual discussions, all sever her
from his affections. The fact that she does not get pregnant
and that he continues to have affairs elsewhere proves how
little her beauty and sexuality can do for her in Wharton's
version of a French marriage. In one of the final ironies
of the book, Undine finds herself trapped by "extreme
domesticity" (*CC*, 485); she felt "the impossibility of
breaking through the mysterious web of traditions, conventions, prohibitions that enclosed her in their impenetrable
net-work" (*CC*, 516). Her ideal of "domestic intimacy"
placed her at the center with all others surrounding her
and catering to her desires. What she learns in France
is that the domestic or relational self is not the center,
but rather a part of an intricate group, woven like her
husband's tapestries into patterns of beauty and grace as
well as utility.

Undine's story, unlike Lily's, does not end in tragedy
because the heroine is incapable of tragic insight. She
believes in remarrying the billionaire version of Elmer
Moffatt that she is trading up, but the reader understands
that her financial "success" is a social "fall". The novel
depicts the rags-to-riches tale as sham. The pioneer quest
to return east, the "call of the Atlantic", ends ironically
in Undine's final deal, her remerger with Moffatt, triggered
by "the instinctive yearning of her nature to be one with
his" (*CC*, 568). Wall Street and Fifth Avenue unite in
a frightening image that we see, not through Undine's
glance into a mirror, but rather through the eyes and sensibilities of Ralph Marvell's son, who has been schooled
by his French stepfather Raymond de Chelles. He feels

an "iron grasp" on his heart and a "rage of hate" (*CC*, 589). Undine and Elmer unite in a marriage of like minds. Passionless and controlled, they embody the customs of their culture:

> Here was someone who spoke her language, who knew her meanings, who understood instinctively all the deep-seated wants for which her acquired vocabulary had no terms; and as she talked she once more seemed to herself intelligent, eloquent, and interesting. (*CC*, 536)

The final irony of the novel is that Undine does find community, not in the leisure-class worlds of Old New York or Europe, among those whose manners, customs and rituals she had aped, but rather in the *nouveau riche* culture of the Nouveau Luxe Hotel, among other *arrivistes* from the obscure Midwest who have likewise heard the "call of the Atlantic". For all her competitive bullying and demanding, Undine simply moves in a circle; she never gets "beyond" the world of her youth, rather its inhabitants follow her as fellow "pioneers". She "fits" into their company and triumphs over them by fitting so well. "At last she was in her native air again, among associations she shared and conventions she understood; and all her self-confidence returned as the familiar accents uttered the accustomed things" (*CC*, 557).

5 *The Age of Innocence* and the Bohemian Peril

They had simply, as Mrs Welland said, "let poor Ellen find her own level" – and that, mortifyingly and incomprehensibly, was in the dim depths where the Blenkers prevailed, and "people who write" celebrated their untidy rites. It was incredible, but it was a fact, that Ellen, in spite of all her opportunities and her privileges, had become simply "Bohemian."

– Edith Wharton, *The Age of Innocence*

In 1920 Columbia University awarded the Pulitzer Prize for literature to Sinclair Lewis for his novel *Main Street*, but in a back room quarrel the Board of Trustees overturned the jury's decision and gave the Prize, by default, to Edith Wharton for *The Age of Innocence*. She was, as her biographer R.W.B. Lewis notes, the first woman, and only the third person, to win that honor. Although she accepted the prize and the thousand dollar check, she was appalled by the last-minute switch. Wharton replied to Sinclair Lewis's congratulatory letter:

As for the Columbia Prize, the kind Appletons have smothered me in newspaper commentary; & when I discovered that I was being rewarded – by one of our leading Universities – for uplifting American morals, I

89

confess I *did* despair.

Subsequently, when I found the prize shd really have been yours, but was withdrawn because your book (I quote from memory) had "offended a number of prominent persons in the Middle West," disgust was added to despair. (*Letters*, 445)

In the eyes of the trustees, it was the American novel of 1920 that best presented "the wholesome atmosphere of American life and the highest standard of American manners and manhood."

How did it happen that her third long study of New York society so baffled the trustees that they read a different novel than Wharton believed she had written? Embedded in the answer, of course, are the questions that engage reader-response theorists. The trustees, a group of successful business people, identified with the hero Newland Archer, bought his speech about "duty" to his wife and family without the irony Wharton intended and concluded, rather smugly, that she had validated their own social customs and values. Newland Archer denies his desire for an exotic American expatriate, Ellen Olenska, and upholds the social status quo by heeding the "bond" or covenant between him and his "tribe". Although he loves Ellen, he remains faithfully with his wife May Welland, the embodiment of Old New York values. In relinquishing his adulterous desire and honoring his long married life, Archer concludes that although he has lost "the flower of life", he has gained the dignity that comes with fulfilling his "duty": "After all, there was good in the old ways" (*AI*, 347).[1] Reading the novel as a love story about the solid, if stolid, American marriage, the Columbia Board of Trustees found Wharton's message sanguineous and pronounced the novel morally uplifting.

We might read the story differently by taking into account the ironies of the novel and, especially, by reading the story as one about womanhood rather than manhood.[2] The hero and main focus of the novel is a man, Newland Archer, who is attracted to two distinct and incompatible women. May Welland embodies the character of established Old New York, a safe, rigid, even icy and gravelike society. Ellen Olenska represents an outlying region, an eccentric, Bohemian culture that emanates fire and animates life. The two women function as Archer's muses, evoking conflicting responses. Over the course of the novel, the hero is forced by his passion for both women to consider risky questions about the social position of women. *The Age of Innocence* is a novel about womanhood because the plot turns on the Woman Question puzzled out by a male protagonist.

Wharton's novel, like *The House of Mirth* and *The Custom of the Country*, is a study of community in American culture. Her characters, both male and female, are inextricably bound to "the customs, manners, culture" of their social group. The Archer/Welland marriage unites the two tribes which dominate New York society. Newland's clan, the Archer–Newland-van-der-Luydens, devote themselves to "travel, horticulture and the best fiction" and May's, the Mingotts and Mansons, to "eating and clothes and money" (*AI*, 34). That might be reason enough for the marriage to work well; the tribes have in fact intermarried numerous times, bringing together the quasi-artistic and the openly-materialistic worlds. The difference between the two groups is negligible enough that in such a union the couple would always be able to rely on the suitability of the match.

Around the edges of Old New York, the "slippery pyramid" of the social élite, in an "unmapped quarter" lurk fantastic characters who ignore its rituals, tastes and opinions. "Long-haired men" and "short-haired women" do what to Old New Yorkers seems inexplicable: they *winter* in Newport, vacation in the tombs of Yucatan, give parties for black men, chat with the Goncourts, Maupassant, and Mérimée, scatter books across the drawing room, and lodge in "*des quartiers excentriques*" among an eclectic array of dressmakers, bird-stuffers, and "people who write" (*AI*, 68, 74).

In earlier Wharton novels, those who threaten the shape and values of established wealth are crass materialists, men and women who hope to rise socially as well as economically by aping the established culture and thereby bullying their way up the slope to the pinnacle of social power. Simon Rosedale, Undine Spragg, Elmer Moffatt all launch assaults on Fifth Avenue which threaten the nascent aristocratic order. *The Age of Innocence*, too, has its financial interlocutor, Julius Beaufort, whose lack of probity in business evokes the ire of Old New York. The real threat to established patterns of life and thought in this novel, however, comes not from business but from Bohemia, a culture that lies outside the lethargic and colorless society of the élite. In its proximity, the Bohemian clan challenges Old New York's hold on its most intelligent, imaginative, sensitive members.

It is Ellen Olenska who comes to represent this third tribe. Under the tutelage of the outrageously nonconforming Medora Mingott, the child Ellen had been reared in a European atmosphere that allowed gaudy clothes, but more importantly "high color and high spirits" (*AI*, 60). Like "a gipsy foundling" the dark, uninhibited child had unsettled the old ladies by asking "disconcerting questions", making "precocious comments" and possessing "outlandish arts". Her education had been what Old New York considered "incoherent": "drawing from the model" and playing the piano with "professional musicians". Only in the rigid, repressed, restricted community of the American élite would such obvious advantages be considered liabilities. Ellen has been allowed to learn about the real world of art and music.

Little wonder that the flat, unimaginative culture in New York should find such genuine training "foreign" and therefore threatening.

As an adult, Ellen continues to dress as she pleases: 'Why not make one's own fashion?" she asks rhetorically (*AI*, 74). Her sitting room is unlike any other woman's, with slender tables of dark wood, a Greek bronze, a stretch of red damask with "Italian-looking pictures in old frames", a vase with only two Jacqueminot roses (when fashion called for a dozen), a vague scent of Turkish coffee and ambergris and dried roses in an air different from any Newland Archer has ever breathed.

Her education, especially the idea that she has had an education, confounds the hero. Newland, in his youth, had read Ruskin, Vernon Lee (perhaps even her review of Gilman, although he only partially understands the feminist analysis), P.G. Hamerton and Walter Pater on art, but they had not prepared him to understand Ellen Olenska's selection of paintings (*AI*, 71). As an adult, he pores over Herbert Spencer, Alphonse Daudet, George Eliot's *Middlemarch* and fantasizes about "the intimacy of drawing rooms dominated by the talk of Mérimée (whose *Lettres à une Inconnue* was one of his inseparables), of Thackeray, Browning or William Morris" (*AI*, 103). In Ellen's drawing room Archer finds works by Paul Bourget (Wharton's good friend), Huysmans and the Goncourt brothers (*AI*, 104). She has, apparently, had an affair with M. Rivière, a French tutor who does indeed live in a *real* world where people talk to Mérimée, Maupassant and the Goncourts. Ellen's husband has, likewise, filled their home with artists and writers. Her education has been first-hand, not vicarious as most of Newland's has been. Her choice of art and selection of books illustrate her intellectual independence and aesthetic sensibility.

In one of the novel's extended ironies, Ellen returns

to America after living most of her life in Europe and
marrying a Polish nobleman and hopes to rejoin her Old
New York family, to embrace the customs, rituals, tastes,
values of her relatives. She feels, with a tinge of exagger-
ation, that in the unhappiness of her marriage she has died
and in her return to New York she has awakened in
"heaven".

The truth is that she has returned because she has left
her husband and learns that to escape her economic dependence on him, she must find a new place to live and money
to support herself. She had married Olenski under French
law and therefore forfeited her own money; he holds all
the economic power and she, by legal design, is reduced
to what Lee and Gilman call "economic parasitism". To
extricate herself from her marriage, she must figure out
a way to make a living. Like Lily Bart and Undine Spragg,
she learns that the easiest course for a woman is to marry
a wealthy man and, like Lily, she comes to realize how
difficult it is to resist that dependency. She comes to
New York to win the support of her familial "tribe", a
group that does not countenance divorce in any case. They
find her "elopement" with Rivière immoral and her
plan to divorce foolhardy. Without their support, in the
form of an allowance from her grandmother Catherine
Mingott, Ellen finds it very difficult to live an independent
life.

Her education, experience, training have all constructed
a very different woman than American culture has produced. We are invited throughout the novel to measure
the distance between Ellen and her cousin May Welland.
Left on her own, Ellen seeks out the community she knows
and understands: "They had simply, as Mrs Welland said,
'let poor Ellen find her own level' – and that, mortifyingly
and incomprehensibly, was in the dim depths where the
Blenkers prevailed, and 'people who wrote' celebrated
their untidy rites" (*AI*, 260). The "gipsy" child becomes

the "Bohemian" adult, her relational self seeks the atmosphere she knows. Her tribe, with its "untidy rites", lies
outside the clans that make up polite, that is to say tidy,
society. It comprises a real community of thinkers, artists
and writers.

The novel reverses the situation in *The House of Mirth*,
where the heroine Lily Bart is distracted from her goal
of marriage by the hero Lawrence Selden and his "republic
of the spirit". *The Age of Innocence* places the hero in
Lily's position; instead of thinking only of a socially-
sanctioned marriage, he is distracted by a freer opportunity. He is to marry the woman his mother would have
chosen, a suitable bride for a leisure-class man, a woman
who will carry out, to the letter, the social form he was
trained to admire and respect. Rather than living happily-
ever-after, however, Newland Archer is attracted to the
free spirit of Ellen Olenska. Her presence calls into
question all his socially-sanctioned desires and sours all
his well-laid plans for domestic happiness. His goal, like
Lily's, is the goal of the romantic hero to get "beyond"
society:

> I want – I want somehow to get away with you into
> a world where words like [adultery] – categories like
> that – won't exist. Where we shall be simply two human
> beings who love each other, who are the whole of life
> to each other; and nothing else on earth will matter.
> (*AI*, 290)

He pleads with Ellen to elope with him to a region beyond
society where they might share an autonomous existence
outside the parameters of their communities. Ellen, who
has lived most of her life outside New York, understands
that the self is always relational. Only in romantic adventure is there a region beyond community where a soul
might live unfettered by the social "web". Unlike

Lawrence Selden who urges the heroine into flight, Ellen rationally considers the consequences. "Oh, my dear – where is that country? Have you ever been there?" Ellen chides him (*AI*, 290). Of course, he hasn't or he would know what Ellen knows: once the train stops in Boulogne or Pisa or Monte Carlo, there is a community waiting. They would still have to find a hotel and live among people, only in a society that is "smaller and dingier and more promiscuous."

Rivière, who has helped Ellen escape from her husband, gives a version of Selden's "republic of the spirit" speech. He talks to Newland about "moral freedom", the ability "to look life in the face" and not bend to necessity, but rather hold to one's own ideas. "You see, Monsieur, it's worth everything, isn't it, to keep one's intellectual liberty, not to enslave one's powers of appreciation, one's critical independence" (*AI*, 200). That freedom is worth "living in a garret for" he concludes. However, it is true that the tutor finds it difficult throughout the novel to earn his way. Newland Archer desires this world, especially in the form of a beautiful woman, but he is incapable of making the sacrifices necessary to become a member of that tribe. Like other American heroes, Newland wants what his name suggests, some "new land" or territory outside the "web" of his culture, beyond the constraints of his community in New York.

Ellen's point is that the territory always has a social context; there is no land beyond the group. What her "republic of the spirit" represents is another community, one which lives on ideas and art, not on money, fine clothes and good food. That Bohemian peril truly threatens Newland because to move to that territory would mean changing his whole life.

The hero has been accustomed to the attraction of womanly beauty and sexuality, but nowhere in his training had he encountered female intellect, imagination, inde-

pendence and aesthetic sensibility, the very traits that titil-
late him. When we first see Ellen Olenska at the opera,
she wears an elaborate costume, the "Josephine look"
including a headdress of diamonds and brown curls
"carried out in the cut of the dark blue velvet gown rather
theatrically caught up under her bosom by a girdle with
a large old-fashioned clasp" (*AI*, 9), a cut "revealing, as
she leaned forward, a little more shoulder and bosom than
New York was accustomed to seeing" (*AI*, 15).

Initially attracted, as the other men are, to Ellen's
exposed bosom, Newland quickly cools to her physical self,
"conscious of a curious indifference to her bodily presence" (*AI*, 242). He even mistakes a "blonde and blowsy"
Blenker girl for her in a curious scene where he makes
love to the wrong parasol. Later he forgets her voice, "that
it was low-pitched, with a faint roughness on the con-
sonants" (*AI*, 230). When they do meet, he explains that
he continually experiences her anew: "*Each time you
happen to me all over again*" (*AI*, 286). When she flings
her arms about him and presses her lips to his, he pulls
away. Physical passion, the feeling he has been trained
to have for a woman, is not the source of his attraction:
"A stolen kiss isn't what I want" (*AI*, 288), he tells her.
When he last sees her at the dinner party, a ritual marking
her ouster from New York, Newland finds her face "luster-
less and almost ugly" (*AI*, 333) and, at the same time,
loves it more than ever.

At the heart of his dilemma, although he doesn't know
it, is the Woman Question. If a woman does not follow
convention and her abilities and talents develop more in
line with men, who *is* she? As Vernon Lee put it in her
review of Gilman's *Women and Economics*: "We do not
know what women *are*." If passion and sensuality do not
draw the male suitor, what does? Newland Archer, for
all his philosophizing about the essential equality of men
and women, had never before Ellen Olenska considered

the concrete possibilities of his abstractions. In the fiery reality of her presence, not the physical but the intellectual dimensions of her being, Newland must reconsider all he has been taught about women.

His vanity is served a socially correct version of maiden-hood in the "young girl in white", May Welland, with a name that more than suggests youthful health and whole-someness.[3] As Christine Nilsson sings the Daisy Song in the opera *Faust*, May sits "slightly withdrawn", in pink modesty with her hair in "fair braids" and her youthful breasts fastened modestly in a "tulle tucker" (*AI*, 6). Archer has had his sexual initiation in a lengthy and mildly agitating affair with Mrs Thorley Rushworth; their liaison had been "a smiling, bantering, humoring, watchful, and incessant lie" (*AI*, 305) that, as the double standard man-dates, left her tainted and him experienced. Watching his fiancée at the opera, he is excited by her purity and proud of her innocence as his possession:

> "The darling!" thought Newland Archer, his glance flit-ting back to the young girl with the lilies-of-the-valley. "She doesn't even guess what it's all about." And he contemplated her absorbed young face with a thrill of possessorship in which pride in his own masculine initi-ation was mingled with a tender reverence for her abys-mal purity. "We'll read *Faust* together . . . by the Italian lakes . . ." he thought, somewhat hazily confusing the scene of his projected honeymoon with the masterpieces of literature which it would be his manly privilege to reveal to his bride. (*AI*, 7)

His smug male vanity over his supposedly superior social and intellectual position will not go unpunished in the novel.

In the first pages, Wharton's narrator explains to the reader Newland's ambivalence. His vanity desires two conflicting attributes in his future wife: the innocence of the ingenuous and sexually naïve May Welland and the experience of the "world-wise" and sexually accommodating Mrs Thorley Rushworth. "How this miracle of fire and ice was to be created, and to sustain itself in a harsh world, he had never taken the time to think out" (*AI*, 7), the narrator explains, using the dominant and conflicting imagery of the novel. "Some say the world will end in fire", Robert Frost put it, "Some say ice." Newland finds in May Welland that fire and ice in such close proximity lose their power. After marrying and living with his Diana-like May, Newland begins to feel the results: "He was weary of living in a perpetual tepid honeymoon, without the temperature of passion yet with all its exactions" (*AI*, 293). The lesson the hero learns in the novel is that what he thought was manly experience turns out in the end to have been boyish innocence.

As the liberal intellectual he fancies himself to be, our hero is a portrait of an "armchair" feminist. He begins to contemplate radical ideas of sexual equality during the homosocial male rite of smoking cigars after dinner in the library. He argues with the gossiping, priggish Sillerton Jackson over Ellen Olenska's indiscretion with M. Rivière; she has apparently lived with him for a year. Aggravated already by the impression Ellen has made on him, Newland defends her right to live with whomever she chooses: "I'm sick of the hypocrisy that would bury alive a woman at her age if her husband prefers to live with harlots" (*AI*, 42). He seems not to understand his own hypocrisy: if women should be free to have sexual affairs when they choose, why does he refer to the other women as "harlots"? Why, we might also ask, the qualifier "at her age"? Or why should she be free only if her husband fails to be monogamous? Archer, however, skims the surface. His jealousy, spurred on by his cigar, leads him further along the road to sexual equality than he had ever

before wandered. "Women ought to be free – as free as
we are," he declared, making a discovery of which he was
too irritated to measure the terrific consequences"
(*AI*, 42).

Later alone in his own library, comfortably seated in
his familiar armchair, Newland ponders the inconsistencies
between his egalitarian philosophy and the reality of his
upcoming marriage to May Welland. Should she also be
free to find another male if he should follow Count Olenski's example? Smugly certain, early in the novel, that adultery would never be his game, he pursues the imbalance
between genders that has the potential of ruining his
marriage. It all hinges on the double standard, the socially
expected innocence of women and experience of men. May
Welland, in his new analysis, becomes the "terrifying product" of his social code, "the young girl who knew nothing
and expected everything."

But what about the question of compatibility? If he has
had a "past" that he could not have had with her or even
tell her about and if she, by the same code, had "no past"
to tell, then how could they become truly intimate? It's
a good question. Many of their past experiences would
have to remain unuttered, his were indeed unutterable;
they would live "in a kind of hieroglyphic world, where
the real thing was never said or done or even thought"
(*AI*, 45). But when he thought of his ideal marriage, he
posited his mate as his equal partner in experience, intellect
and judgement, an ideal his own social code forbids. The
traits he desires are exactly those that have atrophied in
the female to ready her as a respectable marital commodity. In his musings, much of the conflict comes clear
to Newland:

> He perceived that such a picture [of passionate and ten-
> der comradeship] presupposed, on her part, the exper-
> ience, the versatility, the freedom of judgement, which

she had been carefully trained not to possess; and with a shiver of foreboding he saw his marriage becoming what most of the other marriages about him were: a dull association of material and social interests held together by ignorance on the one side and hypocrisy on the other. (*AI*, 45)

From his armchair he is able to pursue a feminist analysis that he never manages to use to shape his life.

A similar analysis appears in all of Wharton's depictions of marriage; the lopsided education and training of men and women make them, in the end, ill-suited companions. Community fails because women and men have not been trained to know each other nor to live together as equals. In élite New York society the male supposedly desires a young woman without experience or versatility or independent judgment, so that he can assume the paternal role of protector and guide. Her economic dependence is only the material compliment of her moral, aesthetic, intellectual dependence on him.

Newland's dilemma is that "this creation of factitious purity, so cunningly manufactured by a conspiracy of mothers and aunts and grandmothers and long-dead ancestresses"[4] is the product he is supposed to want so that he can, literally and symbolically, deflower the virgin himself. Her experience, both sexual and intellectual, will come from him. That system makes some sense, I suppose, if Newland's goal is to own May Welland, to barter for her and buy her as an acquisition. Most of the courtships in Wharton's novels are couched in such business terms. Newland, however, has a hazy notion that what he prefers is an equal partner, a comrade, not a slave. Reason tells him that May should have been allowed the same freedom he has had to learn about the world so that they might become, in marriage, true equals.

Newland Archer, after his marriage, learns approxi-

mately the same lesson Ralph Marvell does in *The Custom
of the Country*. Initially, both men find the inexperienced
woman attractive because they see the opportunity to
educate her, to wander through art galleries and attend
operas and pore over great books together. But neither
man has thought this through carefully or completely. If
he had, he would understand that once intellectual and
aesthetic abilities have, over the long training of youth,
been allowed, even encouraged, to atrophy, they may
never revive and begin to grow strong. The feet of Oriental
women, bound and broken in youth, cannot be expected
in maturity to grow anew and, even less, to produce an
athlete. So intellect, self-confidence, judgement, authority, all traits encouraged in the male and discouraged
in the female, cannot be expected to grow in maturity after
they have withered in youth. It is true that Ralph and
Newland eventually figure this out, but Wharton makes
them both pay for their vain assumption that they will
be able to educate their women after marriage.

The Archer honeymoon is supposed to begin this Pyg-
malion process; Newland hopes to show May the best of
European culture, complete with a tour of the Italian
Lakes. Instead he discovers May is as "morbidly" interested in clothes as his sister Janey is. Her athletic prowess,
likewise, asserts itself, making mountaineering and swim-
ming more appropriate for their time together than Italian
landscapes and masterworks of literature. That is to say,
May doesn't unfold, at his touch, into his creation, rather
she continues to expand her own tastes and talents. "There
is no use in trying to emancipate a wife who had not the
dimmest notion that she was not free," Newland concludes, reverting easily into "his old inherited ideas" (*AI*,
195).

Had he ventured farther along this route, he might have
reconsidered his own notions about "freedom". May, after
all his efforts, does exactly as she pleases or, more accur-

ately, she continues to perform those social customs and to hold those tribal beliefs that she inherited from her culture. While Newland supposes that he is the patriarchal ruler of his household, his life is shaped, controlled, circumscribed by the force of his community. May Welland Archer's boldest move is her premature announcement of her pregnancy to Ellen Olenska – news that both women understand will make the adulterous elopement of Ellen and Newland unthinkable. The pregnancy is proof that despite his passionate words to Ellen, Newland continues to have sex with his wife. But more than that, a pregnancy means the extension of the family, an institution jealously protected by the larger community.

Ellen is unwilling to break that taboo, even though she loves Newland. But more is going on with Ellen Olenska than the hero understands. He would like to exchange one woman for another. She, however, searches for ways to direct her own life. Without money, she is economically dependent on her husband or her clan.

In truth, Ellen is able to use her threat to the Archer marriage to convince her grandmother Catherine Mingott to give her enough money to live an independent life in Paris. In a sense, both women get the life they want or, more precisely, the life best suited to them. May saves her marriage, raises a family and dies heroically nursing her sick child. Ellen finds comfortable quarters in the Faubourg St Germain, in the shadow of the Hôtel des Invalide (in the same area Wharton lived for many years in Paris).[5] She doesn't have to return to her oppressive marriage, nor does she have to manage an adulterous life with her lover. Certainly, her quiet life in Paris, filled with Bohemian artists, musicians, thinkers, writers, is preferable to that allowed her other literary sisters, Anna Karenina or Emma Bovary or Edna Pontellier.

The irony that Newland Archer feels but never quite sees is that the social community of economically sub-

jugated women generates a power of its own. Eccentric
women parade through *The Age of Innocence*, invading
the rarefied world of Old New York society, capturing
attention at operas, parties and weddings. The Duke of
St Austrey pilots the notorious Mrs Lemuel Struthers, "a
tremendous black-wigged and red-plumed lady in over-
flowing furs" (*AI*, 79), into a private party. "Bold" and
"brazen" she wants to "know everybody who's young and
interesting and charming" and gathers them at her Sunday
soirées. Julius Beaufort delights in the company of Fanny
Ring, "a golden-haired lady in a small canary-colored
brougham with a pair of black cobs" (*AI*, 85). The heroine
Ellen Olenska has been raised by the most fantastic of
the lot, her Aunt Medora Mingott, "a wild dishevelment
of stripes and fringes and floating scarves" who flutters
into rooms "festooned and bedizened" (*AI*, 207).

We might expect these female apparitions to function
in the novel merely as colorful background, oddly-
costumed caricatures of "fallen" women. Yet they provide
the only source of energy in Old New York. In the novel's
tension between innocence and experience, between fire
and ice, these wildly arrayed females represent experience
and fire. They animate an otherwise enervated society.

Even the Matriarch of polite society, Catherine "the
Great", began her career as a colorful Spicer of Staten
Island, "with a father mysteriously discredited, and neither
the money nor position enough to make people forget it."
Yet she gained her position by allying herself with "the
head of the wealthy Mingott line" (*AI*, 13). Once established in Old New York, she audaciously broke the rules
by marrying her daughters to "foreigners" and building
"a large house of pale cream-colored stone (when brown
sandstone seemed as much the only wear as a frock-coat
in the afternoon) in an inaccessible wilderness near the
Central Park." In perhaps the most wonderful physical
description in all of Wharton's fiction, the reigning Cather-

ine Mingott, in old age, has acquired an "immense accretion of flesh":

> A flight of smooth double chins led down to the dizzy depths of a still-snowy bosom veiled in snowy muslins that were held in place by a miniature portrait of the late Mr Mingott; and around and below, wave after wave of black silk surged away over the edges of a capacious armchair, with two tiny white hands posed like gulls on the surface of the billows. (*AI*, 28)

Her double chins and billowing body, like the cream-colored house, are signs of her resistance to genteel, leisure-class norms; she has indulged in gluttony as well. The interior of her house, as we would expect in a Wharton novel, expresses her independence of mind; as she aged and found mounting stairs impossible, she established both her sitting room and bedroom on the ground floor, an act that "startled and fascinated" her visitors who saw the propinquity of rooms as an ironic "stage-setting" for scenes of adultery. Catherine Mingott's money and social power prevent her critics from voicing disapproval.

All of these women have, in one way or another, worked around the constrictions of the female social position. Mrs Struthers, for example, made her way on beauty and sexuality but also apparently on hard work and perseverance; beginning her "career" as saloon-girl, she went on to model for "Living Wax-Works" until the police broke it up and later for Lemuel Struthers' "shoe-polish posters", coming out of that deal as his wife. Her energy and interest in good music and gay society, coupled with her husband's money, finally places her at the heart of New York entertaining. Likewise, the infamous Fanny Ring "profoundly agitated" New York society by flaunting her affair with Julius Beaufort; yet eventually, after his wife's death, Beaufort marries her and legitimizes their daughter Fanny

Beaufort, the "bastard" child who will dazzle and marry
Newland Archer and May Welland's son Dallas in the next
generation.

Ironically their son Dallas, as the product of a newly
evolved generation of American youth, finds the elaborately encoded, secretive world of his parents' generation
absurd. "Dash it, Dad, don't be prehistoric" (*AI*, 355)
he blurts out during his open discussion of Newland's
passion for Ellen Olenska. Newland, it turns out, has never
put his liberal ideas into action but has instead lived a
"shy, old-fashioned, inadequate" life. His passion for
Ellen Olenska reifies into a secular "relic", a "chapel"
beyond the real world in which his life was actually lived.
Like Lawrence Selden, Newland is satisfied, not with the
flesh and blood woman, but rather with a romantic fragment: "It's more real to me here than if I went up" he
concludes (*AI*, 361). Ellen's husband has been dead for
several years at the novel's close and May has been dead
for two; Newland Archer was only fifty-five when she died,
leaving him plenty of time for "a quiet harvest of friendship, of comradeship" with Ellen Olenska. Yet ironically
he doesn't write or visit her, rather his son sets up the
would-be "date" that ends the novel.

What Newland never understands in his poignant self-
assessment is that for all his armchair feminist musings,
he never really wanted comradeship with a woman at all.
His inertia allows him a long marriage to a woman very
distant from him. His remote "worship" of Ellen Olenska
gave him an even more distant relationship with her, at
the same time that it precluded a greater intimacy with
his wife. Moreover, in relinquishing Ellen, he gave up her
world as well. The Bohemian peril, a world of independent
ideas and artistic expression, threatens him as much as
it does Old New York. One wonders, at the novel's end,
what energy and promise Ellen's story holds. By leaving
the Archer marriage intact, Wharton frees her other

heroine to create another kind of life. Ellen Olenska maintains an economically and intellectually independent life, so radically free that it scares our hero away. Surely that peril, the Bohemian female alive and well in a Paris apartment, is not the story that captured the attention of Columbia's Board of Trustees.

6 *The Mother's Recompense:* Spectral Desire

What the ghost really needs is not echoing passages and hidden doors behind tapestry, but only continuity and silence. For where a ghost has once appeared it seems to hanker to appear again; and it obviously prefers the silent hours, when at last the wireless has ceased to jazz.

– Edith Wharton, *Ghosts*

Desolation is a delicate thing.

– Shelley, *Prometheus Unbound*

Thank you ever so fondly for taking the trouble to tell me *why* you like my book. . . . No one else has noticed "desolation is a delicate thing," or understood that the key is there.

– Edith Wharton to Margaret Terry Chanler

Edith Wharton claimed to be a ghost-feeler, not a ghost seer, someone she considered "a rare bird". To feel ghosts, she argued, one must sink into "the warm darkness of the prenatal fluid", wander in regions beneath reason.[1] It is in such "primeval shadows" that a writer and a reader may meet to create by mutual agreement the sensations and divinations that suggest an otherwise impalpable form.

In the modern jazz age, Wharton feared that the ability
to enjoy the ghost tale had faded; movies, radio, photo-
graphy had all produced a glaring, noisy world devoid of
shadows, lurking presences, haunting impressions.

   Modernist writers went after ghosts, dragging them out
into the open. Their characters were not haunted by phan-
toms but rather possessed by traumas, neuroses, even psy-
choses. Experimenting with points of view and
fictionalizing subjective reality, modern writers like James
Joyce and Virginia Woolf sought to recreate the workings
of the subconscious mind. Wharton dismissed modernist
linguistic and formal experiments as "sterile word
patterns". After reading Joyce's *Ulysses* (1922), for example, she protested to her friend Bernard Berenson: "I had
already tackled Ulysses & cast it from me" (*Letters*, 461).
The fragmentation of detail seemed to her merely "the
raw ingredients of a pudding," not pudding itself. "I shall
never believe that the raw material of sensation & thought
can make a work of art without the cook's intervening."
In *The Writing of Fiction* (1925) Wharton publicly discussed her opposition to what we now call "modernism".

> This attempt to note down every half-aware stirring of
> thought and sensation, the automatic reactions to every
> passing impression, is not as new as its present exponents
> appear to think. It has been used by most of the greatest
> novelists, not as an end in itself, but as it happened
> to serve their general design ... but they have never
> been deluded by the idea that the subconscious – that
> Mrs. Harris of the psychologists – could in itself furnish
> the materials for their art. (12–13)

The supposed "free association" of images or "stream of
consciousness" seemed to Wharton only the imposition
of another type of pattern, one that remained incoherent
or arcane. The modern desire for "formlessness" suggested

to Wharton a lack of "creative abundance" and a tendency toward "pure anarchy in fiction".

As a social historian, a literary anthropologist, a novelist of manners, Wharton depicted characters within an external, objective world in "some recognizable relation to a familiar social or moral standard" (*WF*, 14). That is to say, Wharton depicted the relational self, the individual enmeshed in the social "web". One way of giving outward, somewhat palpable form to inner emotions and psychological states is to dress them up as ghosts. Edith Wharton preferred that genre, one she used many times during her long writing career. Two of her last ghost stories, "The Pomegranate Seed" and "All Souls" are, in fact, among her best short stories. Many of her novels, as well, contain ghostly elements: the "word" drifting between Lawrence Selden and Lily Bart after her death, for example, or the lurking cat in *Ethan Frome*. And one novel, *The Mother's Recompense* (1925), while not strictly speaking a ghost tale, does rely on ghosts for its meaning. Viewing the spectral nature of her desires, the heroine Kate Clephane comes of age in the novel, or rather comes to middle age.

In spite of its conventional form, *The Mother's Recompense* is an unconventional retelling of the incest story from the point of view of a woman, here an aging mother. Although Wharton's protagonists long to get beyond their original community, to create an autonomous version of themselves, they find that in spite of their struggle they are, in essence, a relational self, bound inextricably to the culture that has produced them. Lily Bart, for example, cannot become a Gerty Farish nor can Undine Spragg, for all her supposed social movement, become a French noblewoman nor can Newland Archer, for all his reading and fantasizing, become a Bohemian.

The incest theme fascinated Wharton, I would argue, because it is a metaphor for the phenomenon I am discussing. That is to say, incest represents the powerful pull of the initial community, parents and family, on the individual. Ethan Frome, for example, marries a version of his mother; Zeena is seven years older than Ethan and had nursed his mother before her death. His attraction to her embodies an incestuous desire. Likewise, Charity Royall, in *Summer*, marries her adoptive father. Both Ethan and Charity are poor, inarticulate, yet consumed by the desire to get beyond their meager lives in the Berkshire mountains. Wharton depicts their desire for escape but places them both back home with their quasi-parents, a cruel fate. Her point, however, is that individuals are tied to their initial culture. The act of freeing oneself from that bond is difficult, indeed nearly impossible in her fiction.

The most disturbing scene of incest that Wharton wrote was not published in her lifetime. The "Beatrice Palmato" fragment that first surfaced in R.W.B. Lewis's biography is a graphic description of oral sex between a father and his newly-married daughter:

> ... suddenly his head bent lower, and with a deeper thrill she felt his lips pressed upon that quivering invisible bud, and then the delicate firm thrust of his tongue, so full and yet so infinitely subtle, pressing apart the close petals, and forcing itself in deeper and deeper through the passage that glowed and seemed to become illuminated at its approach ...
>
> "Ah – " she gasped, pressing her hands against her sharp nipples, and flinging her legs apart.[2]

The daughter's pleasure is so intense that Gilbert and Gubar in *Sexchanges* argue that Mr Palmato is "a paradigm of the *illicit* father, the father who refuses to surrender his daughter to the socioeconomic system represented by the institution of marriage but instead releases her back into the polymorphous eroticism of childhood."[3] That's a difficult argument to make given the other details of the story: the mysterious suicide of the elder daughter after she returns from a convent to live with her parents, the insanity of the mother and her attempt to kill her husband, and the eventual suicide of Beatrice herself.

We might reverse the interpretation and read the father's incestuous desire as a manifestation of the patriarch's inability to relinquish ownership of the daughter. The sexual appetite and expertise of the father destroy all of the women. Beatrice's obvious enjoyment of the coupling itself suggests that however abusive the father may be, the daughter ambivalently longs to be reunited with him; on a metaphorical level, the daughter yearns for home, her initial community.[4] The fragment, never meant to be published in the story itself, depicts the intensity of the bond between parent and child, the desire for reunion.

Wharton worked on the Palmato story in 1918 and 1919, according to her biographer Cynthia Griffin Wolff,[5] slightly before she wrote The Mother's Recompense, a novel about the desire of a mother to recouple with her daughter, in a sense, to reconnect the prenatal bond. Most often psychologists and novelists delineate the detachment between parent and off-spring from the child's point of view; psychosexual stages of "normal" childhood development chart the movement of the child away from home. Instead of focusing on the detachment from the child's point of view, Wharton examines what happens at the other end of the umbilical cord. How does the mother detach from the child, especially from a daughter? Nancy Chodorow's Reproduction of Mothering argues that breaking that bond between mother and daughter is much more difficult than between mother and son. We might expect that female story to be more powerful than the usual Oedipal or Electral patterns of the heterosexual bond.

Wharton transforms the suggestively homosexual incest story into a heterosexual tale, an inversion of the Oedipal myth.[6] Although Kate Clephane, the mother, desires reunion with her daughter, Anne, the daughter desires marriage to her mother's former lover, Chris Fenno, a man about fourteen years younger than Kate. No doubt for the sake of conventional sensibilities, Wharton converts the lesbian attraction into a heterosexual struggle between mother and daughter for a young man. What if, Wharton is asking, we reconsider the Oedipal story from Jocasta's point of view. What must the aging mother feel when she realizes that her lover will become her son, here her son-in-law if not in fact? It is this *ménage à trois*, a mother, her daughter and their lover, that constitutes the slightly displaced incest tale.

Moreover, Wharton self-consciously submerged the theme in "primeval shadows", repressing it in her heroine. As she explained her tactic to her friend John Hugh-Smith:

> I felt, in writing it, all the force of what you say about the incest-element, & its importance in justifying her anguish – but I felt it wd be hardly visible in its exact sense to *her*, & wanted to try to represent the business as it seemed to her, culminating in the incest-vision when she sees the man holding Anne in his arms. (*Letters*, 480)

Had Wharton chosen the technique of "modernist" writers, she would have presented the drama as the stream of thoughts in Kate Clephane's consciousness. Instead she wrote what she herself characterized as "an old-fashioned novel". "I was not trying to follow the new methods," Wharton explained to Hugh-Smith. She wanted to give Kate Clephane's repressed incestuous desire for both her daughter and her would-be son-in-law a more palpable form. In the murky region of unconscious desire, the ghosts in the novel tread.

On the surface, it is a novel of manners, a commentary on social change in America. Old New York is depicted in exactly the same way Wharton has drawn it in her earlier novels; a small, secure, smug world where women find themselves, by necessity, economically and intellectually dependent on men. To get beyond the claustrophobic, unimaginative atmosphere of élite society is the goal of many of Wharton's other protagonists.

This novel, however, significantly varies the usual pattern by allowing the heroine to do just that: Kate Clephane gets "Beyond!" Suffocated by the social restrictions of Old New York, the heroine, at twenty-seven, had abandoned her husband and three-year-old daughter and gone off with a lover to explore the larger world, where she had taken several more lovers, drifted through Europe and had done as she pleased. Eighteen years later, her ex-husband and his mother having died, Kate is invited by her daughter Anne to return to New York, to take up the world and role she had once escaped. As soon as Anne is free to be reunited with her mother, she brings Kate back to New York; later in the novel she hopes her mother will marry an old family friend Fred Landers and thereby restore a version of the family she had lost as a young girl. The novel is only tangentially Anne's story; the focus is Kate's.

Wharton's original version of the Clephane marriage and divorce was entitled "Disintegration" (1902), a project she worked on in 1902 and abandoned after writing eighty pages.[7] As the title suggests, the fragment was to have been her first novel about the ills of American society. Both the early fragment and the later novel, *The Mother's Recompense*, treat the subject of divorce, the breakdown of the family caused by the woman's abandonment of husband and child. The early work begins with the departure of the mother and sympathizes with the daughter and husband. The later novel, however, begins with the mother's return to the daughter and empathizes with the mother.

What is finally enlightening about reading the two works

together is that they suggest a progression in Wharton's thinking. She moves from daughter to mother or from the concerns of youth to those of middle age, and from husband to wife or from the paternal to the maternal point of view.

"Disintegration" tells the story of abandonment from the child's point of view and, in dialogue, from the father's, but only through an unreliable intermediary are we privy to the mother's perspective. Wharton's sympathies are least with the adult woman. From the first page, Alice Clephane (Wharton changes her name to Kate in the novel version) is clearly the villain. Her departure changes life completely for her young daughter, who desperately misses "the continent known as Mamma". Domestically the mother's withdrawal heralds the disintegration of the household, as the title suggests. The loss of mother for Val (in the novel she becomes Anne) is cataclysmic, marked by the sudden absence of the nursery fire, her lessons, her supper. No mother meant an entry into a male world, devoid of orris-scented cushions, drawing-room flowers and fires, afternoon door-bells with glossy-headed gentlemen, tea-trays, ladies in dazzling motors, pink candle-shades, warmth and light and flowers, leaving in their place rice-pudding and mutton and a sense of her father's growing distance from her; he is only close to her for a year (there is little of the Electra impulse in their relationship), and much of that time he is ill.

While Val's story registers the disintegration of the household, Henry's emphasizes the disintegration of Old New York and, therefore, American society. Henry Clephane (his name is John in the novel) is the prototype of Wharton's male romancers: Lawrence Selden, Ralph Marvell and Newland Archer. He had planned a life apart from the materialistic world around him where his discrimination might shine like a moral light-house. That moral light, however, did not shine for Alice Clephane whose extravagant spending – like Mrs Bart's and Undine

Spragg's in later novels – sent her husband into debt and, by necessity, into business. In spite of his concessions, Alice left with another man for crudely utilitarian reasons. As one of the characters, Maud Dulacey, explained it, to abandon one's family for Tillotson Wing was like eloping with a check-book.

When Wharton returned to the story of the Clephane divorce she told an altogether different story, one that empathizes with the woman who had to flee her marriage in order to survive:

> She had left Anne when Anne was a baby of three; left her with a dreadful pang, a rending of the inmost fibres, and yet a sense of unutterable relief, because to do so was to escape from the oppression of her married life, the thick atmosphere of self-approval and unperceivingness which emanated from John Clephane like coal-gas from a leaking furnace. (*MR*, 16)

Wharton uses the imagery of labor; "a dreadful pang", "a rending of the inmost fibres", even "a sense of unutterable relief" all powerfully suggest the initial separation of mother and fetus. Yet Kate had to leave because she "couldn't breathe" in such coal-thick air. Unfortunately she didn't fare any better with Hylton Davies, the wealthy man who spirited her away from Old New York on his yacht. His proprietorship "asphyxiated" her as well. What she desired, although she couldn't articulate it, was economic and intellectual independence, not the "parasitism" that was her lot with both husband and lover. What that freedom cost her was her relationship with her daughter.

Her elopement became simply a more tawdry and less secure version of her marriage. Her life, in fact, is a version of Ellen Olenska's in *The Age of Innocence*. Wharton here tells the story of a woman who escapes from Old New York and invents a new life for herself. Kate, unfortuna-

tely, is not as savvy as Ellen about the workings of the
world nor as responsive to literature and art. She lives
in the world Ellen describes for Newland Archer:

> "Oh, my dear – where is that country? Have you ever
> been there?" she asked; and as he remained sullenly
> dumb she went on: "I know so many who've tried to
> find it; and, believe me, they all got out by mistake at
> wayside stations: at places like Boulogne, or Pisa, or
> Monte Carlo – and it wasn't at all different from the
> old world they'd left, but only rather smaller and dingier,
> and more promiscuous" (*AI*, 290)

This has been Kate Clephane's fate. When Wharton came
to tell the story of the woman alone, outside the traditional
demarcation of feminine identity – not as a wife nor an
active mother – she chose the story of a relatively un-
enlightened woman.[8] Given her limitations, however,
Kate manages her own life fairly well in a series of inexpen-
sive places, with a "circulating library, a mild climate, a
few quiet bridge-playing couples" (*MR*, 17).

Over the years she has written several letters, trying
unsuccessfully to reclaim her daughter; once she freed herself from her husband's tyranny, she longed to live quietly
with her child. After reading *Anna Karenina*, Kate had
even planned an aborted midnight visit to Anne's nursery.
Eventually, she accepts her lack of power to reclaim her
child. Unlike Tolstoy's heroine, however, Kate never
becomes so alienated and disillusioned that she contem-
plates suicide. Rather she muddles through, drifting and
adjusting to her fate.

Her desire for her daughter fades during her affair with
Chris Fenno. She was thirty-nine, at the time, and he perhaps twenty-five. The youthful lover, who had no economic
advantage over her, filled her "soul's lungs" with air, gave
birth to her "real self" (*MR*, 18). Smitten by his "flashing

play of intelligence", Kate believes she has found her "soul
mate". He, however, loves gambling casinos and rowdy
crowds, the "blue of noise and glare and popping corks"
(*MR*, 19). The affair is short lived, leaving Kate with the
sense that being abandoned by a young lover has caused
"the bitterest pain she had ever suffered." The two painful
episodes of her life, her abandonment of Anne and Chris's
of her, collapse into a single struggle with the ghosts of
her past, the scene of the novel proper.

On the surface landscape, Wharton paints a portrait of
the clash in manners and morals between pre-war and post-
war American culture. In the horrific new age of the 1920s
Kate Clephane sees the "millennium where the lamb of
pleasure [has lain] down with the lion of propriety" (*MR*,
63) and where the fresh blunt face of youth is "as unexpres-
sive as a foot-ball" (*MR*, 83). Wharton records her heroine's ambivalence: "Much as Kate Clephane had suffered
under the old dispensation, she felt a slight recoil from
the indifference that had succeeded it" (*MR*, 62). She had
left to avoid old proprieties, but ironically her absence
has allowed her to cling to the old ways as Old New York
has shifted to the new. One of the first lessons the heroine
learns is that getting literally "beyond" New York has not
freed her from her early training. She, ironically, becomes
the spokeswoman for the very social order she thought
she had escaped. Yet amid the sociological study, ghosts
begin to appear:

> As Kate Clephane stood among them, going through
> the mechanical gestures of greeting and small-talk, she
> felt so tenuous and spectral that she almost wondered
> how she could be visible to their hearty senses. (*MR*,
> 229)

Although New York society cannot see her as a ghost,
she understands the "spectral" nature of her being.

On a deeper level, as Kate's mental state suggests, the novel is a psychological study. We are asked to examine what such social changes have done to the heroine and her sense of identity. In the defiance of youth, Kate Clephane had longed to get beyond society, to find her individual essence, her identity outside social attachments and conventions, the "web of customs, manners, culture." Kate's story suggests the difficulties of that desire. To exist outside one's relations to the world is to deny the self. Kate has had nearly twenty years to sever herself from the past, create her own present, invent her future.

When the two worlds, the past and the present, collide, Kate loses her sense of self. Over the course of the novel she must find her new identity by understanding her associations and finally by accepting the reality that her identity is the pattern of her relationships. Her desire to reunite with her abandoned daughter and her youthful lover both represent Kate Clephane's desire, in middle age, to see herself as young again. To have an identity, she must see how over the course of her life, her further attachments have detached her from her youth. That is to say, Kate must learn how the intervening years have had a hand in shaping who she has become, a middle-aged woman, expatriated in Europe.

"Disintegration" calls attention to the personal loss of an abandoned child as a sign of the social loss of the surrounding society. The loss most foreign to Edith Wharton in 1902 belongs to the mother. Alice Clephane becomes the agent of a social force that threatens not only her daughter and husband, but also New York society. She acts from base motives, especially her lust for money and therefore shows no pain, no remorse, no loss of her own.

In the later version of the story, however, the disintegration has relatively little to do with the daughter and the surrounding society, who for the most part have developed in spite of the mother's desertion. Rather the real disintegration involves the losses Kate has suffered, not merely socially, but psychologically. Actually, "disintegration" no longer works as a title because the new story is really about reintegration. The real focus of the novel is Kate's search for her new identity. If she left New York to wander through Europe for eighteen years, who is she when she returns? Her quest is to retrieve and repattern the fragments of her life over those years to answer that question.

"*She*, Kate, was only forty-two ... yes, forty-two .... Or, goodness, was she actually forty-five?" (*MR*, 10–11) The anxious heroine begins the novel counting and recounting on "impatient fingers" and calling her maid for a mirror in order to settle the question of age. When she receives a telegram, she hopes it is from her former lover Chris Fenno saying, "Take me back" (*MR*, 8). What she gets instead is a message: "Mrs. Clephane dead" (*MR*, 9). The telegram announces the death of her mother-in-law, but ironically Kate Clephane is dead as well, at least the old version of her self is dead. A second telegram, this one from her daughter Anne, does say in essence, I will take you back: "I want you to come home at once" (*MR*, 12). But it is her youthful daughter, not her youthful lover, who wants her back.

In spite of her confusion, the reader knows that eighteen years have elapsed, that Anne is now twenty-one; and Kate, although she denies it, is forty-five. Because of her confusion over time, both past and present, Kate continues to live with the three-year-old daughter she left, and the twenty-seven year old woman she was when she left New York; and she will have to come to live with herself and her daughter as adults. To that cast, we must add the abandoned husband John Clephane, who has died in the intervening years.

The oddest part of the puzzle is the former lover, Chris Fenno, who is now about thirty. Their affair had happened before the war and in that broader conflict apparently news of it had not passed to her friends in France, nor to her relatives and friends in America. That point is important to the credibility of the plot. For the story to work, the reader must suspend disbelief (the plot's reliance on coincidence makes that difficult at times) and accept that Chris and Anne later met while he was convalescing from a war injury and she was a volunteer at an army hospital during World War I.

Further we must believe that he did not know that Anne was Kate's daughter (at least, not at first) and that, as her mother had, Anne also fell in love with Chris. When Kate returns to her daughter, it does not take long for the inevitable reunion with her former lover, now to be son-in-law (if Anne is to have her way). Kate is haunted by a new moral dilemma. Should she tell Anne about her affair with Chris in order to prevent their marriage or should she remain silent forever?

Read this way, the novel might easily be dismissed as a melodramatic and sentimental work. But the contemporary reviewers for the most part agreed that *The Mother's Recompense* is one of Wharton's best novels. As H.S. Gorman put it, "It is a tribute to her cleverness that she has skirted the low beaches of sentimentality throughout and kept well within the somewhat tempestuous sea of a passionate imbroglio that is distasteful in itself, but which becomes, as a matter of fact, an affair of lifted tragic intensity."[9] How does Wharton "skirt" the low beaches?

The ghostly elements in the story allow Wharton to wander outside the usual confines and expectations of realism. When Kate returns to New York and meets the adult version of her daughter Anne, what she really sees is a version of herself: "yes, there was her whole youth, her whole married past, in that small pale oval" (*MR*, 36). That vision sets the pattern for virtually every other encounter in the novel. All characters are in some way ghostly versions of Kate.

Lilla Gates, for example, is a flapper version of the social rebel Kate once fancied herself. Lilla, at one point, had "come to grief" (*MR*, 60), but the social scandal had been avoided, and Lilla remained within the tribe, an "outlawed daughter" with "dyed hair, dyed lashes, drugged eyes and unintelligible dialect" (*MR*, 64). Later in Central Park, Kate spies Lilla lingering in the path, a sight that calls up "old associations". She remembers herself on such furtive missions in her own youth. "Was it her own young figure she saw fading down those far-off perspectives?" (*MR*, 106) she asks herself. But Kate resists the association with her own past: "She owned no kinship with that unhappy ghost" (*MR* 106). In serene middle age Kate wants no return to her troubled youth.

To see her own age, Kate must see herself not in Lilla Gates but in Lilla's mother Enid Drover. As Kate looks down the dinner table, she sees Hendrik Drover as "the ghost of John Clephane" and, therefore, his wife Enid as a ghostly self-image, "if she had conformed to the plan of life prepared for her, instead of turning from it and denying it" (*MR*, 253). In such "grotesque fancies" Kate searches for an identity.

Complicating the "ghost story" in the novel is Anne's relationship with Chris, and Kate's disorientation over her own relationship to her daughter and her former lover. When she first returns to Anne, Kate sees not only the adult daughter, but also the ghost of the abandoned three-year-old. In her attempt to retrieve their lost intimacy, to repair the rupture of separation, even to regain the prenatal state, Kate's desire embodies a form of lesbian incest:

> She thirsted to have the girl to herself, where she could touch her hair, stroke her face, draw the gloves from her hands, kiss her over and over again, and little by little, from that tall black-swathed figure, disengage the

round child's body she had so long continued to feel
against her own, like a warmth and an ache, as the ampu-
tated feel the life in a lost limb. (*MR*, 37)

Indeed, her longing for the child, for their complete reunion, prevents Kate from seeing herself as separate from
her daughter: "Kate felt as if they were two parts of some
delicate instrument which fitted together as perfectly as
if they had never been disjoined – as if Anne were that
other half of her life, the half she had dreamed of and
never lived" (*MR*, 76). Her abandonment of her young
daughter has prevented the natural detachment from the
child that would have taken place over the eighteen years;
consequently, Kate still feels their prenatal intimacy, longs
to reunite with her daughter in that primordial ooze. That
incestuous desire to repair their initial bond calls for
ghostly embodiment.

Anne, who never learns about the affair between Kate
and Chris, fights for her mother's approval of the marriage,
while Kate must fight not only her daughter, but also
several ghostly versions of herself. In Anne's passionate
rebellion, Kate sees the ghost of herself at Anne's age.
When Kate battles the whole family, who have sided with
Anne, she sees her new self as a ghost: "under the surface-
rattle of her thoughts a watchful spirit brooded haggardly
on the strangeness and unreality of the scene" (*MR*, 231).
As she confronts Anne's jealousy and anger at her mother's
attempts to prevent the marriage, Kate's identity nearly
vanishes completely: "as if her whole self had passed into
the young body pressed pleadingly against her" (*MR*, 235).

Her personality dissolves, as well, into Chris Fenno's:
"And, in the mad phantasmagoria, there was Chris himself, symbolizing what she had flown to in her wild escape;
representing, in some horrible duality, at once her sin and
its harvest, her flight and her return" (*MR*, 255). Wharton
employs the young Chris Fenno to bring the incest theme

to the surface. Chris functions as a male stand-in for Anne, displacing the desire Kate feels for her daughter, giving it a heterosexual, rather than homosexual cast. Kate Clephane desires her daughter *and* her lover; she feels "tenuous and spectral" in her longing for both.

Like Jocasta, Kate must finally see the full truth, for her that her lover will become her son, that he belongs to youth not to middle age. It is the female quest for truth that interests Wharton, not the male; it is, therefore, Jocasta, not Oedipus, who must learn to see. Images of the eye, of seeing, of shutting the eyelids to hold an image and prevent a new one run throughout the novel. The truth "burns" into Kate's "eye-balls" (*MR*, 274). The climax of her quest for truth comes when the past, present and future merge into one powerful image, a scene of spectral desire that Kate must see as well as feel. With the ghost of the young Anne before her, Kate enters her daughter's bedroom. She sees first Anne's narrow virginal bed, then the wedding dress, and finally Anne and Chris in a passionate embrace. That final confrontation with their youth and her age makes Kate feel again "like a ghost":

> Then a furious flame of life rushed through her; in every cell of her body she felt that same embrace, felt the very texture of her lover's cheek against her own, burned with the heat of his palm as it clasped Anne's chin to press her closer. (*MR*, 278)

In the many levels of incestuous desire, Kate yearns for her daughter, but more for her own youth, especially in the touch of youth as she had experienced it with Chris. The "furious flame of life" is associated in the scene with youth, a ghostly presence to Kate who is, after all, a middle-aged mother. Such powerful sensations obliterate Kate's identity.

Where then is Kate's true self? She hovers ghostlike

over the wedding ritual. And she could then finally accept a new self, the middle-aged mother and mother-in-law, by marrying Fred Landers, who represents a version of John Clephane with none of the personal drawbacks of the first husband.[10] A second marriage would have placed her very near the spot where she would have been had she not left her husband and daughter.

Instead, Kate returns to her old life as a nomadic expatriate. It is only there, among the associations of the last eighteen years of her life that she can finally exorcise the ghosts of the past. Kate learns in the novel what Henry Clephane, the hero of the first version of *The Mother's Recompense*, already knew: humans live by a rut of habit that works well as long as the bounds are set. Henry is forced out of his rut by his wife's departure; but Kate breaks out on her own. To break out of the bounds of one's "customs, manners, culture" is to lose one's identity. She also comes to see, as Ellen Olenska put it, that once the train stops in Boulogne or Pisa or Monte Carlo, there is a new community waiting. That is to say, Kate learns that the self is relational, that she is the middle-aged woman she has become over the intervening eighteen years.

Ironically during her exile, while she wished for a return to her old self, she was all along unwittingly constructing a new one, made up of the fragments of values she carried away with her and the experiences she has had along the way. In that configuration, her return to New York left her ghostlike, without a sense of self. Only her return to France could reunite her with her true identity, in France "she had begun to be aware that she was slipping back without too much discomfort into the old groove" (*MR*, 329). Kate Clephane is the sum of her accumulated experiences: her youth in Old New York and her middle age in expatriate Europe. She is not, as Lily Bart feels herself to be, "expatriate everywhere". Her home, the place she

finds most comfortable, is Europe. Like Ellen Olenska,
Kate Clephane returns there, among the community she
has adopted.

Reintegrating all of her past selves into the rut of her
present one allows Kate her "recompense", meager as it
may be. Wharton's title has been a difficult one for critics
to interpret. Some contemporary reviewers, she complained to her friend Margaret "Daisy" Chanler, believed
that Kate's recompense was Fred Landers's offer of
marriage (*Letters*, 483). The *Saturday Review* critic
argued that the novel was flawed because it ought to have
ended tragically; "*ought to!*" Wharton added. Wharton
bemoaned her fate with such critics and complained bitterly to Chanler that they could not discover what she had
intended. For her the novel's key was in her epigraph from
Shelley's *Prometheus Unbound*: "Desolation is a delicate
thing". That could mean, as Cynthia Griffin Wolff
believes, that Kate Clephane essentially got what she
deserved, perpetual exile, for refusing to accept Landers's
offer of marriage in the end and to rejoin her native community as a middle-aged wife.

However, another clue to understanding the novel's ending is Wharton's dedication: "My excuses are due to the
decorous shade of Grace Aguilar, loved of our grandmothers, for deliberately appropriating, and applying to
uses so different, the title of one of the most admired of
her tales." Adeline Tintner points out that Aguilar had
been popular with the generation of women in Wharton's
grandmother's time for writing novels that became
manuals of a sort for mothers and daughters; *The Mother's
Recompense* was written in 1847. Aguilar was a domestic
novelist, an upholder of "the cult of domesticity", a
believer in the possibilities for happiness in traditional
female roles. A mother's "recompense", her novel posits,
is that her dedication to her daughters throughout life will
translate into their remembrance of her in the generations

following her death. The mother is to lead her daughters into marriage and motherhood, as they will, in turn, lead their daughters.

If Grace Aguilar is a "shade" from Wharton's past, the presiding influence on her grandmother and mother, it is in this novel, with its ironic title, that Wharton exorcises that literary ghost. Although Wharton agreed with domestic novelists that the self develops in and is defined by the community, she questioned the obligatory roles for women established by custom. In her novel, marriage and motherhood are not the "recompense" at all. Kate Clephane left her husband and child, and later rejected marriage to Landers and to another expatriate suitor – "Marry him? God forbid!" (*MR*, 336) – and she has not been in any way eager to assist her daughter into marriage.

Quite the opposite is true. Kate Clephane's "recompense" is an understanding of her "desolation", her place in society as a woman outside the traditional roles that Aguilar celebrated. She is not Mrs John Clephane nor is she Mrs Fred Landers; she is Kate Clephane. In her return to Europe, she reembraces her expatriate self. As Vernon Lee noted. "We do not really know what women *are*": that is the dilemma for the modern woman, the novel suggests. Wharton draws for us a portrait, not of a young lady, but of an aging woman, who comes to recognize and accept the delicate nature of her life in middle age. Once Kate Clephane comes to that knowledge, her ghosts disappear, retreat again into the primordial ooze. Inwardly, Kate "would never have known she was more than twenty," but outwardly she must accept her age, though she "winced a little at being so definitely relegated to the rank where she belonged" (*MR*, 298–9).

7 Edith Wharton and the Critics

> Rather than being the repository of eternal truths, [the classics] embody the changing interests and beliefs of those people whose place in the cultural hierarchy empowers them to decide which works deserve the name of classic and which do not.
>
> – Jane Tompkins, *Sensational Design*

The question of longevity, of enduring literary quality, haunts every writer. What one generation venerates often has little to do with the tastes of the next. Jane Tompkins, in her study of the politics of American canonization *Sensational Designs*, argues that the question of literary survival rests largely with critics and scholars, the powers who keep a writer alive in order to survive themselves. That is to say, the writer must contend with the literary community surrounding her work. The story of Edith Wharton and her critics seems to prove Tompkins's thesis.

Edith Wharton's fate fell first into the hands of the Trinity College historian Gaillard Lapsley, her long-time friend and literary executor, and Percy Lubbock, her one-time friend but long-term foe. Lubbock and Wharton had had a falling out over his marriage to Sybil Cutting some ten years before Wharton's death; and because of that breach, she then refused to write or talk to him. Nonetheless, after her death, Lapsley sought Lubbock's advice about how they might preserve Wharton's life and work.

Lubbock's response to Lapsley's first letter about the

project says much about their treatment of her as a woman and as a writer. Both clearly saw Henry James as the standard against which she was to be judged. In dismissing her correspondence, Lubbock (who had edited James's letters at Wharton's suggestion) wrote that Wharton "was not one to whom letter-writing was a natural overflow of herself and her talk – her letters would give no picture of her, to speak for itself."[1] At least, both men agreed that she did not speak in a characteristically consistent voice, in the way James did. Lubbock, of course, had personal reasons for silencing the voice of Edith Wharton. Instead of publishing her letters, he devised a plan for a memoir, *Portrait of Edith Wharton* (1947), built not around her letters, but letters from her friends "in the form of recollections, reflections, notes of all kinds – freely placed at [his] disposal to be used in any manner that should accord with the design of the book" (vi). Lapsley agreed that letters from others, most of whom were not literary people at all, would be more representative of the writer than her own letters would be. Can one imagine them dismissing Henry James's letters in such fashion? By suppressing Wharton's letters, her own words, Percy Lubbock managed to have the last word (at least for many years).

Not surprisingly, Edith Wharton never quite commands Lubbock's *Portrait* of her. She is cast from the first page as "the dazzling intruder, *la femme fatale*" who barges into Henry James's world, shattering his sense of order, devouring his time and energy. She becomes "the wild woman, angel of devastation", terms the men around her had used. At the same time as he characterizes her destructive force, Lubbock undercuts her as a writer and as a person:

[Henry James] admired her effect in the world – he watched, he presided over it . . . it was as good as a fiction of his own . . . If she was a novel of his own she

did him credit . . . All this was much more than her pretty
little literary talent, the handful of clever little fictions
of her own. (5–6)

Lubbock's portrait of Wharton becomes essentially a
tribute to Henry James: "It was enough, I suppose, that
she was herself a novel of his, no doubt in his earlier
manner" (8). With Lapsley's blessing on Lubbock's pro-
nouncements, Edith Wharton emerged after her death as
a marginal writer and woman. Lubbock's memoir served
the next generation an Edith Wharton who was cold,
austere, snobbish as a woman, and in spite of her hawk-like
presence, not much of a writer.

During her lifetime, however, Edith Wharton had many
tangible successes. Her first important novel, *The House
of Mirth* sparked in its first year, according to her editor
William C. Brownell, "the most rapid sale of any book
ever published by Scribner."[2] From her meticulously kept
records of her earnings from 1904 to 1914, we know that
her writing brought her about $32,000 in 1906 (perhaps
a quarter of a million dollars today), and that about $27,000
of that sum came from royalties on *The House of Mirth*.
Along with money came praise from close friends, like
Howard Sturgis, who proclaimed that except for Henry
James, "I think you are head and shoulders above any
other writer of fiction of the present day in English."
Among the letters came approval from Hamlin Garland
and Henry James, who saw Lily Bart as "big and true".
That and subsequent novels drew praise from William
Dean Howells, Joseph Conrad, F. Scott Fitzgerald, and
Sinclair Lewis, to name a few of the male writers of her
age who valued her work.

The reviewers universally praised her graceful, fluent
style as subtle, plastic, seductive. *Review of Reviews*
claimed that *The House of Mirth* was "worked out in a
manner to stamp the writer a genius, and give her name

a place in the history of American literature." *Saturday Review* concurred that it was "one of the few novels which can claim to rank as literature." The novella *Madame de Treymes* (1907), like *The House of Mirth*, exemplified, according to Mary Moss, an "unimpeachable distinction of style" and therefore "stands entirely above criticism." Vernon Atwood agreed that it was "an absolutely flawless and satisfying piece of workmanship." Later novels, *The Reef* (1912), for one example, seemed like "carved ivory"; and *Summer* (1917), for another, was "carved like a gem". Even after World War I, when many critics saw her sharp eye failing, Henry Seidel Canby wrote of *The Age of Innocence* that it was a "fine novel, beautifully written, 'big' in the best sense" and "a credit to American literature."

Despite increasingly negative reviews during the 1920s, Carl Van Doren called *The Glimpses of the Moon* (1922) "lucid, balanced, aware, easy, alive." And R.D. Townsend claimed it "sustains its author's recognized position among the leaders in American fiction." One of her greatest admirers Arthur Hobson Quinn believed Wharton to be "the foremost living novelist writing in the English language" in the 1920s. In celebrating her literary talent and its probable longevity, he questioned, "For after all which of *us* are as truly alive as Lily Bart, as Ethan Frome, as Ellen Olenska, as May Welland? And which of us will live as long?"[3]

Of her autobiography Edward Sackville-West wrote in 1934: "Over these admirably written and exquisitely well-mannered pages hovers the peace of riches that are not only material." Throughout her lifetime, at least with some critics, Wharton remained a major American writer.

In spite of her recognized genius as a writer, Wharton met with considerable negative criticism. The biggest complaint during and after her lifetime was with her pessimism. Her portraits of individuals enmeshed in a social net of "customs, manners, culture" produced unhappy endings, more often than not. As Wharton herself noted, Americans want a tragedy with a happy ending. Even then, it took not so much the death of Lily Bart, as the maiming of Ethan Frome and Matty Silver to enrage the critics. In an interesting irony, the *American Library Association Booklist* pronounced the novel about life in a small New England community "too depressing to be recommended for any but large libraries." *Outlook* followed by hoping that "when Mrs. Wharton writes again she will bring her great talent to bear on normal people and situations."

Such admonishments fit the age in which she lived, but surprisingly the charge of cruelty continued after her death. In 1938, Q.D. Leavis measured Wharton's talents against those of Henry James in an effort to answer the question of her talent: "The final question then is, what order of novelist is she? – i.e., not how permanent but how good?"[4] Leavis believed that not even Wharton's "greatest admirer" would proclaim her a great novelist. "I think it eventually becomes a question of what the novelist has to offer us, either directly or by implication, in the way of positives." By that standard, it comes as no surprise that she called Wharton's talents "remarkable if not large-sized," just as Leavis preferred George Eliot's positives to Flaubert's negatives.

Edith Wharton, Leavis believed, suffered from "the absence of poetry in her disposition." In 1956, Lionel Trilling, puzzling over his dislike of *Ethan Frome*, agreed with Q.D. Leavis that Wharton's "strong if limited intelligence" as a writer combined with "a limitation of heart" as a woman. He called her treatment of Ethan Frome, her creation of "that grim tableau" of Ethan, Matty and Zeena, gratuitous suffering, created out of Wharton's cruelty.[5] Irving Howe, in his collection of Wharton criticism in 1962, had the same difficulty with Wharton's world view. He noted in her fiction "the inexorable disarrangement of everything we seek through intelligence and will to arrange" (*Edith Wharton: A Collection of Critical Essays*, 16–17). He also charged her with lacking "the vocabulary of happiness".

What these critics used as a criterion for greatness was a novelist's (especially a female novelist's) willingness to present, at least to some degree, the brighter side of life. It is true that Wharton dwelt on the darker side, as did Hawthorne, Poe and Melville before her, and Dreiser, Crane and Norris in her own time. Could it be her gender that made her pessimism so unpalatable for critics? Moreover, her pessimism and sense of the inexplicable disarrangement of all we seek to order is modernist in impulse, linking her to Joseph Conrad, James Joyce, Virginia Woolf and other "modernists", in spite of her criticism of their linguistic and structural experimentation.

The bitterest attack on Wharton came from Alfred Kazin, who considered her gender in a harsher light:

> It was a condescending resignation that evoked in her the crackling irony that smarted in her prose; it was the biting old dowager of American letters who snapped at her lower-class characteristics.[6]

Kazin's portrait of Wharton reveals a strong bias against women, especially against older and wealthier women. Not only her gender but also her social class damned her in his eyes. His prejudices echoed Vernon Parrington's attack on Wharton in 1921. In condemning her social class, Parrington joked, "She is as finished as a Sheraton sideboard."[7] He argued her "distinction is her limitation" because "if she had been forced to skimp and save and plan, she would have been a greater and richer artist." Aggravated by her intelligence, coupled with her opportunities, Parrington found, "She unconsciously irritates because she reveals so unobtrusively how much she

knows and how perfect is her breeding." As Kazin would
later, Parrington used her age (by 1921 she was nearly
sixty) to dislodge her from the mainstream of American
writers. He placed her opposite "the honest crudities of
the younger [male] naturalists."

Other critics, however, have eyed her pessimism from
a personal and psychological perspective. Lubbock's portrait of Wharton and her portrait of herself had left readers
and critics alike with little sense of her personal life. As
late as 1964, before her papers were opened at Yale
University, Marius Bewley discussed "Mrs. Wharton's
Mask". "The dearth of information that exists concerning
Mrs. Wharton's real personality has not been fortunate
for her critical reputation", he noted.[8] He spoke for a
group of critics who have theorized that her fiction "seems
projected from some deep center in herself, from some
concealed hopelessness, frustration, or private rage that
we are never allowed to see except at several removes
in the disguising medium of her art."

The opening of the Beinecke Library collection of her
letters and manuscripts, and the accompanying biographies
by R.W.B. Lewis in 1975 and Cynthia Griffin Wolff in
1977 did, as Bewley hoped, provide voluminous details
about Wharton's personal life. For example, they laid open
to public scrutiny scenes of desire, from her pornographic
fragment "Beatrice Palmato", shedding light on the incest
motif that runs throughout much of Wharton's work and
also on scenes of adultery, specifically with Morton Fullerton, that explained, for Wolff, the maturing of Wharton's
fiction. Such inquisitiveness about personal, especially
sexual, matters characterizes much of the direction of bio-
graphical criticism in recent years.

R.W.B. Lewis and Nancy Lewis's *The Letters of Edith
Wharton* (1988) makes available even more detail, in
Wharton's own voice(s), about her personal relationships.
Such unveiling, especially of her letters to Morton Fuller-

ton, first published in *The Library Chronicle* in 1985, would clearly have disturbed Edith Wharton. One has only to remember *The Touchstone* (1900) and the case of the writer Margaret Aubyn, whose love letters are sold after her death by her lover Stephan Glennard, to glimpse Wharton's own horror at the thought of making herself "public property", a commodity for profit. What Glennard faces in the novella are "the divinities who, below the surface of our deeds and passions, silently forge the fatal weapons of the dead." He is haunted by the ghostlike presence of Margaret Aubyn – thinly veiling Wharton's own presence – who presses him to see the injustice of providing to the public a woman's personal letters, revealing her "soul, absolutely torn up by the roots" (67).

Even before the unveiling of the details of her life, critics considered her work as the outpouring of her personal maladjustments. In his "Justice to Edith Wharton" in 1941, Edmund Wilson perceived her work to be "the desperate product of a pressure of maladjustments."[9] He argued that the work between *The House of Mirth* and *The Age of Innocence* is her best for this reason: "It is sometimes true of women writers – less often, I believe, of men – that a manifestation of something like genius may be stimulated by some exceptional emotional strain, but will disappear when the stimulus has passed." Ironically, his "justice" contains a strange view of women, especially women writers. Women are emotional beings; sometimes stress can stimulate their artistic inclinations; but the achievement is not really "genius" and will usually disappear after the stress is resolved.

Echoing Wilson in 1942, Alfred Kazin insisted, "To Edith Wharton, whose very career as a novelist was the tenuous product of so many personal maladjustments, the novel became an involuted expression of self" (*On Native Grounds*, 67). She was only interested in literary fame "to attain by the extension of her powers the liberation she needed as a woman", he concluded, thus she never achieved greatness. Clearly Kazin doesn't see the connection between the woman and her art, nor does he believe that a man might write to gain "liberation" as a man. In a neat, though fathomless, distinction, he separated James from Wharton: "James's need of art was urgent, but its urgency was of the life of the spirit; Edith Wharton's was desperate." For Kazin "the Republic of the Spirit" is closed to leisure-class women – a point, by the way, that Lily Bart understood.

Cynthia Ozick, calling for "Justice (Again) to Edith Wharton" in 1976, discovered that female critics had adopted the maladjustment theory that Wilson and Kazin had both used to explain female art. Ozick singled out Ellen Moers, for example, who in *Literary Women* (a book that all but excludes Wharton) argued that "strong emotion in women, emotion uniquely female, is what will best nourish a female literature."[10] Emotional distress, so Ozick reads such feminists, feeds female talent.

The examination of Wharton's maladjustments as nourishment for her art continued in Cynthia Griffin Wolff's *A Feast of Words*, which begins with the seemingly simple pronouncement: "It is usually easier not to write than to write." Wolff argued that Wharton's early fear of her mother caused repression and frustration that damaged her marriage and limited her fiction. After the death of her mother and amid the unhappiness of her marriage, especially through her affair with Morton Fullerton, Wharton was able to develop sexually. Therefore, her fiction matured as well. Unlike many of the earlier male versions of her life, Wharton becomes a heroine in Wolff's. "And still, by some feat of intellect and passion and will, that nearly extinguished young woman had confronted life and become, if not its master, at least its partner ..." (406). Wolff's work suggests that Edith Wharton might fare better as a writer in the hands of female critics.

It is significant, I think, that studies of women in literature that were written during the 1970s shied away from Wharton. Perhaps influenced by Percy Lubbock's pronouncement that Wharton did not number women among her friends or perhaps offended by Wharton's attacks on the feminists of her day, many female scholars unearthing American women writers left the ground over Wharton undisturbed. Not until Margaret McDowell's essay, "Viewing the Custom of her Country: Edith Wharton's Feminism" (1974) did feminist scholars begin to see her in light of turn-of-the-century female thought. McDowell argued that Wharton's novels were feminist in that they explored the aspirations and deprivations of women in a male-dominated society. Elizabeth Ammons, following this same line, wrote an insistent and useful study of Wharton's "feminism" by placing her work alongside the feminist texts of her day. Edith Wharton wasn't cruel to her female characters, Ammons argued, she was simply depicting with accuracy the lives of women in her time.

> Wharton was never able to write a happy, positive story about the New Woman in America, and she did not fail because she was reactionary or unconcerned ... Attuned to and sympathetic with "the woman question" in her fiction before the 1920s, Wharton was quite capable of creating ambitious, lively young women who want to be New Women ... But the culture, in Wharton's opinion, offers them no means of realizing their dreams. Lily Bart, Justine Brent, Mattie Silver, Sophy Viner, Charity Royall: all end up in bondage to the past not because Edith Wharton was cruel but because the liberation, the "progress," that America boasted of for women was, in her view, a mirage.[11]

Ammon's book suggested a new direction for feminist revisions of Wharton's novels as well as her politics.

The revision of feminist critics reveals a change in the power structure of American criticism, which is, as Jane Tompkins argues, a political act. Underlying so many of the male explorations of a curiously male-dominated American canon is Hawthorne's fear of the "damned mob". Even those men who had previously given Wharton some ground did so because, as E.K. Brown put it, Wharton is able "to transcend the limitations of her sex . . . she is at ease in a man's world."[12]

But more often than not, male critics have tended to see her as the best writer in a fairly fallow field of writers at the beginning of the twentieth century. "By contrast with other writers who were active between 1900 and 1912 she seemed not only remarkably skillful but also unusually certain of her aims . . . but in a very narrow field", Granville Hicks explained in *The Great Tradition*.[13] Edmund Wilson, reiterating the line, argued that in the period from 1905 to 1917, "when there were few American writers worth reading" Wharton was "one of the few . . . who found an articulate voice and set down a durable record" (*The Wound and the Bow*, 172). Henry Bamford Parkes echoed Hicks in *The American Experience* (1947) by acknowledging that

> most of the writers of the time devoted themselves, on a decidedly superficial level, to the problem of politics. Two women, Edith Wharton and Ellen Glasgow, were producing work of finer quality; but each of them dealt with a fragment of ordered society, imbued with traditional standards of manners and morals, in no way typical of the American scene.[14]

The woman's world of social and domestic interaction, as I have argued, has rarely been seen, in discussions of literature, as typical of America. Blake Nevius, writing the first full book of Wharton criticism in 1953, claimed her as "our most successful novelist of manners" but, like Lionel Trilling and Richard Chase, diminished her stature by judging the novel of manners to be "an alien and difficult genre."[15] Viewing American literature, he might well have said an alien and difficult *gender*.

The question over the last decade of Wharton criticism has been her place, not in a male-defined, but rather in a female re-defined literary tradition. How "at ease" is Wharton in a woman's world? Amy Kaplan, in "Edith Wharton's Profession of Authorship" (1986), argued that Wharton belonged at the "intersection" of popular literature, the woman's novel, and realism in "an uneasy dialogue with twentieth-century modernism." That is to suggest that Wharton does not fit easily and completely into any literary movement, at least as those movements have been previously defined.

Shari Benstock in her recent study of women and modernism, *Women of the Left Bank: Paris, 1900–1940*, takes up the task of re-defining modernism through the work of twenty-two women of the period in Paris. Using feminist and deconstructive critical theory, Benstock has sought a new route, one that avoids the conclusions such theorists have made before: "It has been argued that the two practices always arrive at the same conclusions: that the patriarchy represses woman, entraps her, subjects her to its self-enforcing images; that in the patriarchy woman exists under erasure, absent, dispossessed of identity" (7). Rather than repeat that line, Benstock proposes a study of "the difference *within* gender, within the experience of gender; here an alternative reading to woman's predetermined plot offers itself." Such a study, published the same year as Kaplan's article, promises a portrait of Edith Wharton as a realist writer in the modern period in "uneasy dialogue" with modernist experimenters.

Instead Wharton becomes a primitive woman, a missing link, between the nineteenth and twentieth centuries.

Benstock gives us a fictionally-drawn portrait of Wharton
as she first appeared in literary Paris in December 1893
at the door of the well-known writer Paul Bourget (37).
The day is "bleak", the air is chilly, the heroine is dressed
in "somber" clothes. She hides in the "shadows" and
appears "sad", pinched, weighted down, strained and constrained. As though Wharton were some half-human form,
a Neanderthal woman, Benstock explains, "We try to trace
our descent from hers." It is suprising that in a study of
the multiplicity of female voices in the early twentieth
century, Benstock finally consigns Wharton, both the
woman and her writing, to the nineteenth: "Wharton
belonged totally to the nineteenth century, although she
spent thirty-seven years of her life in the twentieth" (86).
Totally? Benstock implicitly, even explicitly, admires the
world of progressive change and radical innovation and
thus leaves Wharton outside the door.

Sandra M. Gilbert and Susan Gubar have, likewise,
begun a study of modernism, a reappraisal of the dialectics
of the age. They focus on the theme of sexual battle, in
a zone they call, from the war metaphor, *No Man's Land*.
Their goal in Volume 2, *Sexchanges*, is to study the changes
in "definitions of sex and sex roles" in three periods they
demarcate as "Victorian ideology of femininity", "anti-
utopian skepticism", and "apocalyptic engendering".

In this scheme, Wharton fits along with Willa Cather
into the second stage of their progressive model. They
write of her, as Percy Lubbock did, as the "angel of devastation", a woman with unflagging energy and hawklike
intelligence who peered skeptically into the realities of her
culture. On the issue of Wharton's ambivalent feminism,
they conclude: "despite all this evidence that Edith
Wharton was neither in theory nor in practice a feminist,
her major fictions, taken together, constitute perhaps the
most searching – and searing – feminist analysis of the
construction of 'femininity' produced by any novelist in

this century" (128). Their pronouncement merely echoes the earlier judgments of Margaret B. McDowell and Elizabeth Ammons. However, their study situates Wharton within the modernist dialogue more acurately than Benstock's has done.

This new situating of Wharton within the boundaries of feminist criticism and the methods of feminist scholarship has elicited an angry response from James W. Tuttleton, whose earlier study *The Novel of Manners in America* had argued that Wharton is one of the six or so best writers in American literature. His recent article, "The Feminist Takeover of Edith Wharton" (1989), maintains that central position for Wharton in the American canon of writers. He argues, as Amy Kaplan has, that Wharton was an "androgynous" writer and quotes Wharton in her letters for support: "'I conceive my subjects like a man – that is, rather more architectonically & dramatically than most women – then execute them like a woman,' so as to provide 'the small incidental effects that women have always excelled in, the episodical characterization, I mean.'"

All of this sounds reasonable enough, yet throughout the article he links several female projects. After the publication in 1988 of Wharton's letters, two former research assistants for R.W.B. Lewis's *Edith Wharton: A Biography*, Mary Pitlick and Marion Mainwaring, wrote in the *Times Literary Supplement* condemnations not only of Lewis's judgment in selecting the letters but also of his use of their material in his 1975 biography.[16] Tuttleton, in his attack, groups Pitlick and Mainwaring, whose article he called "embittered and incoherent ... mean-spirited and condescending, and ... utterly muddled," with Cynthia Griffin Wolff, Elizabeth Ammons, Carol Wershoven and Wendy Gimbel, and with two participants in a 1988 Wharton conference, Elaine Showalter and Wendy Martin, and further with feminists from the general culture, Betty Friedan and Bella Abzug, and finally with

Ms. magazine in what he sees as a conspiracy: "the sorority of feminists" are taking over Wharton criticism. To lose Edith Wharton is hard, but to lose her to a mob of women is apparently too much to bear. We might characterize his response as bitter, condescending, even muddled. He makes no distinction between one critic and another and apparently has not read Benstock or Kaplan.

What such heated rhetoric suggests is that Edith Wharton has become big business indeed. As a female writer, she has had to weather criticism of her gender, morality, intellect and social class, even her mental health. The current battle line is drawn not between Wharton and her critics but between critics themselves. The critics, those with a powerful "place in the cultural hierarchy", struggle for control of Wharton as scholarly and critical property. The very fact that the battle rages is a sign of Wharton's stature. Her resiliency over several generations of ideo-logical literary debate and revision bodes well for her longevity.

Notes

References to Wharton's books are given parenthetically in the text by an abbreviation and a page number. The following is a list of editions cited, along with the abbreviations used.

Fiction:

The House of Mirth (Scribner's, 1905). (*HM*)
The Fruit of the Tree (Scribner's, 1907). (*FT*)
Ethan Frome (Scribner's, 1911). (*EF*)
The Custom of the Country (Scribner's, 1913). (*CC*)
Summer (Appleton, 1917). (*S*)
The Age of Innocence (Appleton, 1920). (*AI*)
The Mother's Recompense (Appleton, 1925). (*MR*)

Non-fiction:

The Decoration of Houses (Scribner's, 1897). (*DH*)
The Writing of Fiction (Scribner's, 1925). (*WF*)
A Backward Glance (Appleton-Century, 1934). (*BG*)
The Letters of Edith Wharton (Scribner's, 1988). (*Letters*)

Notes to Chapter 1

1. Janet Flanner, "Dearest Edith", *The New Yorker*, vol. v (2 March 1929), pp. 26–8.
2. Edith Wharton, "Life and I", in *Edith Wharton: Novellas & Other Writings*, Cynthia Griffin Wolff (ed.) (New York, Library of America, 1990), pp. 1071–96.
3. Carolyn Heilbrun, *Writing a Woman's Life* (New York, Norton, 1988), p. 37.
4. There are two significant biographies, both written in the 1970s, that together recreate Wharton's life. See R.W.B. Lewis, *Edith Wharton: A Biography* (New York, Harper & Row, 1975) for the details of her life, her friends, houses, travels, etc. Also see Cynthia Griffin Wolff, *A Feast of Words: The Triumph of Edith Wharton* (Oxford University Press, 1977) for a psychobiographical portrait of Wharton's personality.
5. Jane Addams, "The Subjective Necessity for Social Settlements",

in *Philanthropy and Social Progress*, intro. Henry C. Adams (New York, T.Y. Crowell, 1893), pp. 12–13.

6. *The Living of Charlotte Perkins Gilman: An Autobiography* (New York, Harper & Row, 1975; 1st pub. 1935), p. 96.

7. Judith Fryer, *Felicitous Space: The Imaginative Structures of Edith Wharton and Willa Cather* (Chapel Hill and London, University of North Carolina Press, 1986), p. 73.

8. Marilyn French, "Muzzled Women", *College Literature*, vol. XIV (1987) no. 3, pp. 219–29. The issue contains nine papers given at the 1987 Wharton Society conference, Edith Wharton at The Mount, including work by Katherine Joslin, Elizabeth Ammons, Cynthia Griffin Wolff, Margaret B. McDowell, Robin Beaty, Rhoda Nathan, Moira Maynard and Annette Zilversmit, in addition to French.

9. For James's letters to Wharton, see also Lyall Powers (ed.), *The Letters of Henry James and Edith Wharton* (New York, Charles Scribner's Sons, 1990).

10. Wharton to Norton, 1 March 1899. The Lewises did not select this and other significant letters to women in their edition, which includes only 300 of the perhaps 6,000 Wharton letters known to be in existence. See my review of *The Letters of Edith Wharton*, R.W.B. Lewis and Nancy Lewis (eds), *Review*, vol. XII (1990).

11. Shari Benstock, *Women of the Left Bank: Paris, 1900–1940* (Austin, University of Texas Press, 1986), pp. 37–70.

12. For a much fuller discussion of Wharton's war work, see Alan Price, "Writing Home from the Front: Edith Wharton and Dorothy Canfield Fisher Present Wartime France to the United States: 1917–1919", *Edith Wharton Newsletter*, vol. V (Fall 1988) no. 2, pp. 1 ff.

Notes to Chapter 2

1. Edith Wharton, "The Great American Novel", *Yale Review*, vol. 16 (1927), p. 652.

2. With the punning of "bonds", I am echoing Nancy Cott's use of the word in *The Bonds of Womanhood: "Woman's Sphere" in New England, 1780–1835* (New Haven and London, Yale University Press, 1977). She has borrowed the pun from Sarah Grimke.

3. For an example of such an argument, see Richard Chase, *The American Novel and Its Tradition* (Garden City, New York, Doubleday Anchor, 1957).

4. Nancy Chodorow, *The Reproduction of Mothering: Psychoanalysis and the Sociology of Gender* (Berkeley and London, University of California Press, 1978), p. 167.

5. Carol Gilligan, *In a Different Voice: Psychological Theory and Women's Development* (Cambridge, Mass., Harvard University Press, 1982), p. 170.

6. Edith Wharton, "Confessions of a Novelist", *Atlantic Monthly*, vol. 151 (Apr. 1933) no. 4.

7. See Amy Kaplan, "Edith Wharton's Profession of Authorship", *English Literary History*, vol. 53 (Summer 1986), pp. 433–57. Kaplan argues that Wharton distances herself from the female domestic novelists of the nineteenth century by viewing her writing as a business not as a part of her other female domestic chores. She goes on to link Wharton, through her work with the architect Ogden Codman, to male discourse. "Rather than simply reject the conventional female realm of domesticity, Wharton appropriates the conventional male discourse of architecture and brings it into the interior space that had consigned women to decorating themselves as one among many ornaments" (444). I agree that Wharton sought to masculinize her fiction by appropriating male discourse, as I detail here, specifically male scientific or quasi-scientific writing.
8. Émile Zola, "The Experimental Novel", in *Modern Literary Realism*, George J. Becker (ed.) (Princeton University Press, 1963), p. 166.
9. Quoted in Becker, 169n.

Notes to Chapter 3

1. Wilbur Cross to Edith Wharton, 28 Oct. 1912, and her response through Anna Bahlmann, 15 Nov. 1912, are both in the Beinecke Rare Book and Manuscript Library, Yale University.
2. Nina Baym, *Woman's Fiction, A Guide to Novels by and about Women in America, 1820–1870* (Ithaca and London, Cornell University Press, 1978), pp. 11–50.
3. Edith Wharton to Sara Norton, 26 Oct. 1906. Quoted in Wolff, *A Feast of Words*, p. 111.
4. Compare Joan Lidoff, "Another Sleeping Beauty: Narcissism in *The House of Mirth*", in *American Realism: New Essays*, Eric J. Sundquist (ed.), (Baltimore and London, Johns Hopkins University Press, 1982), pp. 238–58. Lidoff argues that the novel is a psychological "romance of identity" with the characters and terrain of the novel serving as props for Lily Bart's inner drama. She grants towards the end of her essay that the psychic regression of the heroine into a state of narcissism is forced on her by a society that "provides no female adult role of active responsibility and initiative." Lily's life within that outward society, which I think Wharton describes adequately as a world surrounding her heroine, is the topic of my essay.
5. See Frances L. Restuccia, "The Name of the Lily: Edith Wharton's Feminism(s)", *Contemporary Literature*, vol. XXVIII (1987) no. 2, pp. 223–38. Restuccia reads the novel as a model of feminism(s): first, it contains a "social feminist" analysis of the ills of the female in the repressive society of turn-of-the-century America; second, Wharton's text embodies a "literary feminism" that, like literary texts, resists a final, closed reading. She sees Lily as open, ambiguous, indeterminant, reading her as a deconstructionist theorist (she uses Roland Barthes' *Image Music Text*, translated by Stephen Heath;

New York, Hill and Wang, 1977) might read a "text". Lily is a "plastic", "malleable" heroine who resists the label "victim", a reading that Selden, as a lawyer, wants to give her. Restuccia concludes, "Until the utopia of textualized law, whatever that would be like, feminism has no choice but doubleness – a doubleness that will be destructive to feminism, a source merely of endless interfeminist disputation, until its necessity is taken for granted." My reading, given these terms, contains a "social feminist" reading, except that in the end I also believe that Wharton's text remains open. Wharton, in this novel, has no answer to the Woman Question.

6. Irving Howe, *Edith Wharton: A Collection of Critical Essays* in Twentieth-Century Views Series (Englewood Cliffs, New Jersey, Prentice-Hall, 1962), p. 15.

7. Margaret McDowell, "Viewing the Custom of the Country: Edith Wharton's Feminism", *Contemporary Literature*, vol. 15 (1974), pp. 521–38.

8. See Wolff, *A Feast of Words*, p. 127, where she discusses Lily as an art "object".

9. See Wai-Chee Dimock, "Debasing Exchange: Edith Wharton's *The House of Mirth*", *Publication of the Modern Language Association*, vol. 100 (Oct. 1985), no. 5, pp. 783–92. Dimock lays out the pattern of financial metaphors in the novel. She argues that the central issue in the novel is not sex but exchange and that the "feebleness and limitation" of Lily Bart's supposed rebellion against the morality of the marketplace "attests as well to Wharton's own politics, to her bleakness of vision in the face of a totalizing system she finds at once detestable and inevitable." I agree that Wharton's ambivalence kept her from envisioning another kind of society or even allowing her heroine to make realistic compromises within the system Wharton detests.

10. See Elaine Showalter, "The Death of the Lady (Novelist): Wharton's *House of Mirth*", *Representations*, vol. 9 (Winter 1985).

11. Robin Beaty, "Lilies that Fester: Sentimentality in *The House of Mirth*", *College Literature*, vol. XIV (1987) no. 3, pp. 263–75.

Notes to Chapter 4

1. Judith Fryer argues in *Felicitous Space* (95–116) that *Custom of the Country* is an "urban pastoral" because Wharton sees the city, not nature or the countryside, as the locus of human values. Undine's power threatens urban society, Fryer points out, not because the city *per se* is corrupt, but because Undine brings to it the shallow, unimaginative values of the midwestern prairie. I agree essentially with Fryer's argument although I focus my analysis on Wharton's depiction of the corruption of urban society, not on her lament over the loss of an implicit ideal society.

2. Both Lewis and Wolff argue that Undine is a version of Wharton herself. Her nickname, like Wharton's, is "Puss" and she, like the

of the *Woman Writer in the Twentieth Century: Volume 2, Sexchanges* (New Haven and London, Yale University Press, 1989), p. 166.

4. Both Lewis, see pp. 524–6, and Wolff, *A Feast of Words*, see pp. 379–89, discuss the incest theme in Wharton's work and its link to her own desire for her father's affection. As Wolff puts it: "Just as the little girl's unresolved feelings about her father might affect all subsequent *sexual* relationships, so the same persistent ghost of oedipal uncertainty might resonate in any *cross-generational* relationships."

5. Wolff, *A Feast of Words*, "Appendix: The Dating of the 'Beatrice Palmato' Fragment", p. 407. The fragment itself has no date, and Lewis argues that although her notebook reveals that Wharton had begun to think about the story in about 1920, she may not have written the fragment until 1935.

6. See Adeline R. Tintner, "Mothers, Daughters, and Incest in the Late Novels of Edith Wharton", *The Lost Tradition: Mothers and Daughters in Literature*, Cathy N. Davidson and E.M. Broner (eds) (New York, Frederick Ungar, 1980), pp. 147–56. Tintner argues that the Oedipal triangle is so horrifying to Kate Clephane because she "views the lover as a husband and the coupling of her daughter and the man who represents the husband-figure becomes an incestuous act" (150). I argue that Kate is horrified by the prospect of her lover becoming her son. I also see the incestuous tangle as including the mother's desire to be reunited with her daughter. Tintner interprets, and I think rightly so, Kate's "recompense" as her ability finally to understand her "own identity".

7. Edith Wharton, "Disintegration", 1902, unpublished MS, Beinecke Library.

8. See Marilyn French's "Muzzled Women", *College Literature*, vol. XIV (1987) no. 3, for her attack on Wharton's unwillingness to give her heroines the independent life she herself apparently lived.

9. H.S. Gorman, Review of *MR, New York Herald* (3 May, 1925), 7.

10. See Wolff's analysis of the novel, *A Feast of Words*, pp. 357–70. She argues that Kate is a woman without a past or even a sense of time. In Wolff's reading Kate's refusal to marry Fred Landers is proof of her unwillingness throughout to accept middle age and her proper place in time. I obviously disagree with her reading.

Notes to Chapter 7

For an early version of this chapter, see my article, "Edith Wharton at 125", *College Literature*, vol. XIV (1987) no. 3, pp. 193–206.

1. Percy Lubbock, *Portrait of Edith Wharton* (New York, Appleton-Century, 1947), p. v.

2. Lewis, *Edith Wharton: A Biography*, p. 152.

3. Arthur Hobson Quinn, *American Fiction: An Historical and Critical Survey* (New York, Appleton-Century, 1936), p. 550.

4. Q.D. Leavis, "Henry James's Heiress: The Importance of Edith Wharton", *Scrutiny*, vol. VII (Dec. 1938), p. 261.
5. Lionel Trilling, "The Morality of Inertia (Edith Wharton: *Ethan Frome*)", *Great Moral Dilemmas in Literature, Past and Present*, Robert M. MacIver (ed.) (New York, Institute for Religious and Social Sciences, 1956), p. 37.
6. Alfred Kazin, "Two Educations: Edith Wharton and Theodore Dreiser", *On Native Grounds* (New York, Harcourt Brace Jovanovich, 1942), p. 61.
7. Vernon Parrington, "Our Literary Aristocrat", *Pacific Review*, vol. II (June 1921), p. 157.
8. Marius Bewley, *Masks and Mirrors* (New York, Atheneum, 1964), p. 146.
9. Edmund Wilson, *The Wound and the Bow* (New York, Oxford University Press, 1947), p. 160.
10. Cynthia Ozick, "Justice (Again) to Edith Wharton", *Commentary*, vol. 62 (Oct. 1976), p. 48.
11. Elizabeth Ammons, *Edith Wharton's Argument with America* (Athens, University of Georgia Press, 1980), pp. 48–9.
12. E.K. Brown, "Edith Wharton, The Art of the Novel", in Pelham Edgar's *The Art of the Novel: From 1700 to the Present Time* (New York, Macmillan, 1933), p. 196.
13. Granville Hicks, *The Great Tradition* (New York, Macmillan, 1933), pp. 217–18.
14. Henry Bamford Parkes, *The American Experience* (New York, Knopf, 1947).
15. Blake Nevius, *Edith Wharton* (Berkeley, University of California Press, 1953), p. 9.
16. For details of the feud between R.W.B. Lewis and his former research assistants, see Mary Pitlick, Letter, *TLS*, 30 Dec. 1988–5 Jan. 1989, p. 1443. And also Marion Mainwaring, "The Shock of Non-recognition", *TLS*, 16–22 Dec. 1988, pp. 1394 and 1405. For Lewis's response, see Letter, *TLS*, 17–23 Feb. 1989, p. 165.

Bibliography

Wharton's Novels and Novellas, Chronologically Arranged

The Touchstone (New York, Scribner's, 1900).
The Valley of Decision (New York, Scribner's 1902), 2 vols.
The House of Mirth (New York, Scribner's, 1905).
Madame de Treymes (New York, Scribner's, 1907).
The Fruit of the Tree (New York, Scribner's, 1907).
Ethan Frome (New York, Scribner's, 1911).
The Reef (New York, Appleton, 1912).
The Custom of the Country (New York, Scribner's, 1913).
Summer (New York, Appleton, 1917).
The Marne (New York, Appleton, 1918).
The Age of Innocence (New York, Appleton, 1920).
The Glimpses of the Moon (New York, Appleton, 1922).
A Son at the Front (New York, Scribner's, 1923).
Old New York (New York, Appleton, 1924) 4 vols.
The Mother's Recompense (New York, Appleton, 1925).
Twilight Sleep (New York, Appleton, 1927).
The Children (New York, Appleton, 1928).
Hudson River Bracketed (New York, Appleton, 1929).
The Gods Arrive (New York, Appleton, 1932).
The Buccaneers (New York, Appleton-Century, 1938).
Fast and Loose: A Novelette by David Olivieri (ed.) Viola Hopkins
    Winner (Charlottesville, University Press of Virginia, 1977).

Wharton's Collected Short Stories

The Greater Inclination (New York, Scribner's, 1899).
Crucial Instances (New York, Scribner's, 1901).
The Descent of Man, and Other Stories (New York, Scribner's, 1904).
The Hermit and the Wild Woman and Other Stories (New York,
    Scribner's, 1908).
Tales of Men and Ghosts (New York, Scribner's, 1910).
Xingu and Other Stories (New York, Scribner's, 1916).
Here and Beyond (New York, Appleton, 1926).
Certain People (New York, Appleton, 1930).
Human Nature (New York, Appleton, 1933).
The World Over (New York, Appleton-Century, 1936).
Ghosts (New York, Appleton-Century, 1937).

The Collected Short Stories of Edith Wharton (ed.) R.W.B. Lewis (New York, Scribner's, 1968, 2 vols.).

Wharton's Books of Poetry

Verses (Newport, Rhode Island, C.E. Hammett, Jr., 1878).
Artemis to Actaeon and Other Verse (New York, Scribner's, 1909).
Twelve Poems (London, The Medici Society, 1926).

Wharton's Non-Fiction Books

The Decoration of Houses, with Ogden Codman, Jr. (New York, Scribner's, 1897).
Italian Villas and Their Gardens (New York, Century, 1904).
Italian Backgrounds (New York, Scribner's, 1905).
A Motor-Flight through France (New York, Scribner's, 1908).
Fighting France from Dunkerque to Belfort (New York, Scribner's, 1915).
French Ways and Their Meaning (New York, Appleton, 1919).
In Morocco (New York, Scribner's, 1920).
The Writing of Fiction (New York, Scribner's, 1925).
A Backward Glance (New York, Appleton-Century, 1934).
The Letters of Edith Wharton (ed.) R.W.B. Lewis and Nancy Lewis (New York, Scribner's, 1988).

Selected List of Other Works Cited

Ammons, Elizabeth, *Edith Wharton's Argument with America* (Athens, University of Georgia Press, 1980).
Baym, Nina, *Woman's Fiction, A Guide to Novels by and about Women in America, 1820–1870* (Ithaca and London, Cornell University Press, 1978).
Benstock, Shari, *Women of the Left Bank: Paris, 1900–1940* (Austin, University of Texas Press, 1986).
Bewley, Marius, *Masks and Mirrors* (New York, Atheneum, 1964).
Bloom, Harold (ed.), *Modern Critical Views: Edith Wharton* (New York, Chelsea House, 1986).
Chodorow, Nancy, *The Reproduction of Mothering: Psychoanalysis and the Sociology of Gender* (Berkeley and London, University of California Press, 1978).
Davidson, Cathy N. and E.M. Broner (eds), *The Lost Tradition: Mothers and Daughters in Literature* (New York, Ungar, 1980).
Fryer, Judith, *Felicitous Space: The Imaginative Structures of Edith Wharton and Willa Cather* (Chapel Hill and London, University of North Carolina Press, 1986).
Gilbert, Sandra M. and Susan Gubar, *No Man's Land: The Place of the Woman Writer in the Twentieth Century: Volume 2, Sexchanges* (New Haven and London, Yale University Press, 1989).
Gilligan, Carol, *In a Different Voice: Psychological Theory and Women's Development* (Cambridge, Mass., Harvard University Press, 1982).

Gilman, Charlotte Perkins, *Women and Economics* (New York, 1899).

Gimbel, Wendy, *Edith Wharton: Orphancy and Survival*, Landmark Dissertations in Women's Studies Series, Annette Baxter (ed.) (New York, Praeger Special Studies, 1984).

Heilbrun, Carolyn, *Writing a Woman's Life* (New York, Norton, 1988).

Howe, Irving (ed.), *Edith Wharton: A Collection of Critical Essays* in Twentieth-Century Views Series (Englewood Cliffs, New Jersey, Prentice-Hall, 1962).

Jelinek, Estelle C. (ed.), *Women's Autobiography* (Bloomington and London, Indiana University Press, 1980).

Kazin, Alfred, *On Native Grounds* (New York, Harcourt Brace Jovanovich, 1942).

Kolodny, Annette, *The Lay of the Land: Metaphor as Experience and History in American Life and Letters* (Chapel Hill, University of North Carolina Press, 1975).

Lewis, R.W.B., *Edith Wharton: A Biography* (New York, Harper & Row, 1975).

Lubbock, Percy, *Portrait of Edith Wharton* (New York, Appleton-Century, 1947).

Nevius, Blake, *Edith Wharton* (Berkeley, University of California Press, 1953).

Oldsey, Bernard (ed.), "Edith Wharton Issue", *College Literature*, XIV, 3 (1987).

Lyall Powers (ed.), *The Letters of Henry James and Edith Wharton* (New York, Charles Scribner & Sons, 1990).

Quinn, Arthur Hobson, *American Fiction: An Historical and Critical Survey* (New York, Appleton-Century, 1936).

Sundquist, Eric J. (ed.), *American Realism: New Essays* (Baltimore and London, Johns Hopkins University Press, 1982).

Tompkins, Jane, *Sensational Designs: The Cultural Work of American Fiction, 1790–1860* (Oxford University Press, 1985).

Tuttleton, James W., *The Novel of Manners in America* (New York, W.W. Norton, 1972).

Veblen, Thorstein, *The Theory of the Leisure Class: An Economic Study in the Evolution of Institutions* (New York and London, Macmillan, 1899).

Wershoven, Carol, *The Female Intruder in the Novels of Edith Wharton* (London, Associated University Press, 1982).

Wilson, Edmund, *The Wound and the Bow* (Oxford University Press, 1947).

Wolff, Cynthia Griffin, *A Feast of Words: The Triumph of Edith Wharton* (Oxford University Press, 1977).

Wolff, Cynthia Griffin (ed.), *Edith Wharton: Novellas & Other Writings* (New York, Library of America, 1990).

Index

Addams, Jane, 11, 12
Aguilar, Grace, 126
Alcott, Louisa May, 34
Ammons, Elizabeth, 54, 74, 137, 141
autobiography, 4–7, 18
    female, 4, 6
    male, 4, 5

Balzac, 43
Baym, Nina, 32, 51
Benstock, Shari, 54, 139–40
Berenson, Bernard, 27, 109
Berry, Walter, 10, 19, 22, 27
Bourget, Paul, 93, 140

Cather, Willa, 35, 140
Chanler, Margaret Terry "Daisy", 18, 25, 126
Chodorow, Nancy, 33, 112
Chopin, Kate, 35
Conrad, Joseph, 130, 133
Cooper, James Fenimore, 28
Crane, Stephan, 41, 133

Darwin, Charles, 40
determinism, 38–9, 40–3, 66
domestic novels, 33, 34–5, 39, 51–3, 62, 64–5, 68, 69, 126–7, 139
Dreiser, Theodore, 41, 133

Eliot, George, 93, 132
Emerson, Ralph Waldo, 30, 50

feminism, 53, 54–8, 62, 63, 99–101, 106, 137, 140–1
Fitzgerald, F. Scott, 130
French, Marilyn, 16
Fryer, Judith, 15, 47
Fullerton, Morton, 19–21, 22, 27, 134

Garland, Hamlin, 130
Gilbert, Sandra and Susan Gubar, 21, 27, 54, 111
Gilligan, Carol, 34, 63
Gilman, Charlotte Perkins, 11, 12, 49, 54–8, 62, 64, 69–71, 74, 79, 94, 97
Glasgow, Ellen, 35, 138
Gubar, Susan and Sandra Gilbert, 21, 27, 54, 111

Hawthorne, Nathaniel, 30, 31, 133, 138
Heilbrun, Carolyn, 5, 22
Howe, Irving, 54, 132
Howells, William Dean, 9, 28, 35, 55, 62, 130
Hugh-Smith, John, 113
hysteria, 11–13

incest theme, 110–13, 122–4, 134

James, Henry, 7, 15, 17, 28, 129, 130, 132, 136
Jelinek, Estelle, 4
Jones, Mary Cadwalader "Minnie", 27
Joyce, James, 109, 133

Kaplan, Amy, 139–41
Kazin, Alfred, 133, 134, 135
Kolodny, Annette, 32

Lapsley, Gaillard, 128–30
Lawrence, D. H., 31
Lee Vernon (Violet Paget),
    49, 54–8, 61–4, 69, 93–4,
    97, 127
Lewis, Nancy, 20, 134
Lewis, R. W. B., 10, 17, 19,
    20, 89, 111, 134, 141
Lewis, Sinclair, 89–90, 130
Longfellow, Henry
    Wadsworth, 9
Lubbock, Percy 128–30, 134,
    137, 140

Mainwaring, Marion, 141
McClellan, Dr, 11
McDowell, Margaret, 54, 137,
    141
Melville, Herman, 3, 31, 133
Mitchell, S. Weir, 11, 12, 13
modernism, 109–10, 113, 133,
    139, 140–1
Mount, The, 14–16

naturalism, 38–9, 40–3, 134
Nevius, Blake, 138
"New Woman", 53, 62–3
Norris, Frank, 41, 133
Norton, Sara "Sally", 11,
    18–19
novel of manners, 83, 110,
    113, 139

Ozick, Cynthia, 136

Paget, Violet, see Vernon Lee
Parrington, Vernon, 133–4
Pavillon Colombe, 14, 26
Phelps, Elizabeth Stuart, 34

Pitlick, Mary, 141
Poe, Edgar Allan, 3, 133
Pulitzer Prize, 89–90

realism, 42
romance, male pastoral, 30–2,
    35, 38, 43–5, 50–2, 62, 66,
    68–70, 84–5, 95, 115
Ruskin, John, 93

Showalter, Elaine, 54, 62, 141
Southworth, E. D. E. N., 34
Ste Claire, 14, 26, 27
Sturgis, Howard, 7, 130

tableau vivant, 59, 76
Taine, Hippolyte, 40–1
Tompkins, Jan, 128, 138
Trilling, Lionel, 83, 132
Tuttleton, James, 141
Twain, Mark, 31
Tyler, Royall, 27

Veblen, Thorstein, 56, 73–4

Warner, Susan, 34
Wharton, Edith: life, 1–27
    earnings, 130
    expatriation, 23
    family, 2, 4–5
    houses, 14, 26–7
    hysteria, 11
    marriage, 10
    war work, 23
    writing, 1, 22
Wharton, Edith: works,
    28–127
    Age of Innocence, The, 9,
        26, 36, 42, 45–6, 47,
        89–107, 116–17, 131
    Backward Glance, A, 3,
        26, 43, 54, 131

Wharton, Edith: works—
  continued
  "Beatrice Palmato", 21,
    111–12, 134
  Book of the Homeless,
    The, 23–4
  Buccaneers, The, 26
  Bunner Sisters, The, 9
  Children, The, 9, 26
  "Confessions of a
    Novelist", 39
  Custom of the Country,
    The, 9, 45, 70–88, 91,
    94, 102
  Decoration of Houses,
    The, 13
  "Disintegration", 114–16,
    119
  Ethan Frome, 9, 16, 36,
    45, 47, 110, 111, 132
  Fast and Loose, 8
  Fighting France, 24
  French Ways and Their
    Meaning, 24, 35, 54, 85
  Fruit of the Tree, The, 9,
    16, 36, 38, 42
  Ghosts, 108
  Glimpses of the Moon,
    The, 26, 131
  God's Arrive, The, 26,
    46–7
  "Great American Novel,
    The", 29
  Greater Inclination, The,
    13
  House of Mirth, The, 9,
    16, 36–7, 42, 44, 47,
    49–69, 76–8, 84–7, 91,
    94, 95, 106, 110, 130
  Hudson River Bracketed,
    26
  Italian Backgrounds, 16
  Italian Villas and Their
    Gardens, 16
  Madame de Treymes, 131
  Marne, The, 24
  Mother's Recompense,
    The, 9, 25, 26, 46,
    108–27
  Motor-Flight Through
    France, A, 16
  Old New York, 26
  Reef, The, 16, 131
  Sanctuary, 16
  Son at the Front, A, 24, 26
  Summer, 9, 36, 40, 111,
    131
  Touchstone, The, 14, 135
  Twilight Sleep, 26
  Valley of Decision, The,
    16, 55
  Writing of Fiction, The,
    26, 43, 109
Wharton, Theodore "Teddy",
  10, 21, 22, 27
Wilson, Edmund, 135, 138
Wolff, Cynthia Griffin, 20–1,
  84, 112, 126, 134, 136, 141
Woman Question, The, 49,
  55, 61, 63, 69, 91, 97, 137
Woolf, Virginia, 109, 133
World War I, 23–4

Zola, Émile, 41